Debt and Disorder

Debt and Disorder

International Economic Instability and U.S. Imperial Decline

Arthur MacEwan

Monthly Review Press
New York

Library of Congress Cataloging-in-Publication Data

MacEwan, Arthur.
  Debt and disorder : international economic instability and U.S.
  imperial decline / Arthur MacEwan.
      p.   cm.
  ISBN 0-85345-795-6 : $26.00.—ISBN 0-85345-796-4 (pbk.):$10.00
    1. Debts, External—Developing countries.   2. Debts, External—
Latin America.   3. Debts, External—United States.   I. Title.
HJ8899.M33   1990
336.3'435'091724—dc20   89-13416
                                                              CIP

Monthly Review Foundation
122 West 27th Street
New York, N.Y. 10001

10 9 8 7 6 5 4 3 2 1

For Margery

Contents

List of Tables and Figures

Acknowledgments

The ideas and arguments in this book were developed over a number of years, and I am indebted to many people who gave me comments and criticisms along the way. An initial formulation of parts of Chapter 2 were published in *Science & Society* (Summer 1986), and earlier versions of parts of Chapters 3, 4, and 5 appeared in *Monthly Review* (February 1985, February 1989, and September 1986). I am grateful to the editors of these journals for both their comments at the early stage and their later permission to use the material. Vince Valvano provided very helpful research assistance, and he also gave me numerous useful suggestions on the formulation of my arguments. John Bellamy Foster likewise contributed some valuable advice at the final stages. My debt to Jim Campen is extremely great. He read the entire manuscript, subjecting both the substance of my argument and my presentation to meticulous scrutiny, leading me to make many changes and, I believe, greatly improving the book. Susan Lowes not only did a fine job of final editing, but it is also likely that without her early encouragement this book never would have been written. Finally Margery Davies gave me the support and advice, both direct and indirect, that she does in all my undertakings.

1

International Debt: Crises and Conflicts

In his famous novel *One Hundred Years of Solitude*, Gabriel García Márquez presents a scene in which one of the principal characters, José Arcadio Buendia, has been deemed crazy and is accordingly tied up to the chestnut tree in the courtyard. There he is regularly visited by the priest, Father Nicanor. García Márquez writes:

> On a certain occasion when Father Nicanor brought a checker set to the chestnut tree and invited him to a game, José Arcadio Buendia would not accept, because according to him he could never understand the sense of a contest in which the two adversaries have agreed upon the rules.

The rules of a game define how the system works, what can and cannot be accomplished from the contest, and what kinds of problems will emerge. In economic affairs, as in games, the most important question is how the system works.

During the last two decades, the international economy has been in a state of considerable turmoil. The rapid economic expansion that defined an era in the decades following World War II is over. In its place we have slow economic growth, or relative stagnation. As aspects of this stagnation, we have seen myriad crises of the world economy: inflation and recession, energy crises, sharp exchange rate fluctuations, huge trade imbalances, and, not least, an enormous buildup of international debt.

A massive expansion of international banking activity in the 1970s, taking place out of the public eye, laid the foundation for the debt buildup. Then, at the beginning of the 1980s—in the summer of 1982, to be precise—the third world debt crisis became a public event. By the end of the 1980s, while third world debt difficulties were alive as ever, the huge growth of the U.S. foreign debt had also come into the spotlight.

International debt problems, involving the arcane operations of the world's financial system, may appear abstract and far removed from people's daily lives, but those problems have had severe, pernicious, and very concrete impacts. In the third world, debt problems have increased hunger, illness, and degradation; debt has become the new barrier to progress, dashing hopes and solidifying misery for millions of people. In the United States, when we look at job loss, the growing insecurity of workers, and rising income inequality, we find clear connections to the expansion of this country's foreign debt. International debt problems are, then, real and immediate issues, and the story of international debt is significant because it can help us understand and do something about these very practical matters.

The story of international debt is also a particularly interesting and important part of the larger tale of what has been happening to the world economy. The debt story ties together many aspects of that larger tale of disorder, and in addition it gives us a window through which to see how the world economy is moving. If we tell the debt story properly, it gets us to the roots of international capitalism; we can learn something of how that system works and we can begin to figure out the rules of the game.

We could tell the debt story in another way. We could focus

on the policies that have been followed by governments and bankers, try to determine what "mistakes" were made, and from there attempt to prescribe "correct" policy. Telling the story in this way, we would take the rules of the game for granted. It is like playing checkers in the usual way—not a bad game, but not a very enlightening one either.

Father Nicanor, in García Márquez's fable, becomes disconcerted when confronted with José Arcadio Buendia's approach to checkers. The priest had never seen the game played by putting the rules up for grabs. In a similar manner, economic analysis that does not accept the rules of the game also strikes many people as fanciful, impractical, and irrelevant to figuring out what should be done about a problem. In fact, nothing could be further from the truth. The really serious problems of our economic lives—and the general disorder of the international economy is certainly among the serious problems—have their roots in the way the system works, in the rules of the game. Policy adjustments that leave those rules intact may provide some relief, or they may change the appearance of the problems. If the game continues to work the same way, however, the problems will reappear—perhaps in different form, but they will reappear. International debt, as I shall try to show, illustrates this point rather nicely.

My purpose in this book, then, is to tell the story of international debt and disorder. I also want to suggest what people can do about the disorder of the world economy, a disorder that has brought misery to the lives of millions and threatens disruption on a huge scale. My story implies that if we want to begin to set things right, we must do something about the rules of the game. We need to change basic structures of economic life, both within national economies and in the world economy.

The main line of the story is relatively simple. During the twenty-five years following World War II, capitalism around the world was extremely successful. Particular circumstances allowed fairly rapid economic growth, and that growth combined with the imperial power of the United States to assure a high degree of economic stability. However, by the end of the 1960s the bases for rapid economic expansion and stability had been substantially eroded. Growth slackened in virtually all regions of the system. The ability of the U.S. government and U.S. business to maintain stability declined. The world economy entered an era of relative stagnation and instability.

In their efforts to cope with these new international circumstances, governments and businesses followed a set of policies that engendered a huge buildup of international debt. Third world debt was the early manifestation of this process. By the end of the 1980s, however, U.S. foreign debt had also become a major piece of the story. The problems of the era thus appear today as debt problems, but in fact their origins lie in stagnation and instability. With different policies, the problems might have manifested themselves differently, but disruptions and difficulties would nonetheless have arisen in one form or another.

In the next three chapters, I will set out details of the story. In Chapter 2, I describe how the interaction of international events and U.S. government policies generated major changes in the international financial system. The third world debt crisis grew directly out of the disarray that developed as stagnation set in and U.S. imperialism went on the defensive. Responding to these conditions, the large internationally operating banks proceeded to "push" funds into the third world. In this sense, the debt crisis originated in the central, advanced capitalist countries.

The debt crisis also originated in a "pull" that was based in the economies of the third world. In Chapter 3, which focuses on Latin America, I tell the "pull" part of the story. Latin America's reliance on foreign capital derives from the region's long history of dependence and inequality. Within this structural context, the debt crisis of the current era emerged from the changing relations of class power that were shaped by the long postwar expansion of the international economy, and then by the disarray that accompanied the decline of U.S. imperial power in the 1970s.

In the 1980s, the U.S. government's response to stagnation and imperial decline gave a new twist to the international debt story. In Chapter 4, I describe how the great shift in the international financial position of the United States took place. Entering the decade as the world's principal creditor, the United States dramatically switched, becoming the world's largest debtor and building up a huge trade deficit. Economic expansion was maintained during the 1980s, but only at considerable immediate and potential cost. The U.S. foreign debt is closely tied to the very large foreign trade deficit. So in this chapter I discuss the trade deficit as well as the debt, and argue that trade "dislocation" is the principal way in which debt problems have had their impact on the lives of people in the United States.

Chapters 5 and 6 deal with some of the political questions that have emerged along with international debt. In Chapter 5, I examine responses to the debt crisis in Latin America, posing the questions: why haven't the governments of the region defaulted on their debt? and why have the peoples of the region tolerated continued payment? By answering these questions, I am able to say something about both possibilities and limits on change in the current era.

While in Chapter 5 I write as an outsider, describing events and possibilities in Latin America, in Chapter 6 I turn to the politics of the progressive movement in the United States. Although questions of international finance are far removed from most people's daily lives, there are nonetheless useful ways in which progressive oppositional forces can develop strategies to deal with the debt crisis and other international economic problems. These issues are closely connected to long-standing struggles—anti-intervention struggles, struggles over government spending programs, and struggles surrounding foreign trade and jobs. By emphasizing these connections, we can build a stronger oppositional movement.

In order to take up my story, I must set the stage. So in the remainder of this introductory chapter I will first define the third world debt crisis and then explain the way its political and economic impact has spread through the world system. This impact is the more serious because the third world debt crisis is but one of several financial problems affecting international affairs. The U.S. foreign debt is one of the other major problems, and I will complete this chapter by describing the dimensions of the U.S. debt and pointing out the way its story and the story of third world debt are closely linked.

Although debt problems are global problems, my approach in this book is to focus on the United States and Latin America, particularly the large debtor countries of Latin America. These are the areas of the world where my own political concerns are centered and with which I am the most familiar. Also, the United States and the Latin American countries have played particularly important roles in the development of current world financial problems. Nonetheless, I hope the reader will keep in mind that this book tells only a part of the story of international debt and disorder.

What Is the Third World Debt Crisis?

The "third world debt crisis," as it is usually termed, became a public event in the summer of 1982 when the Mexican government announced that it could not meet its obligations on the debt it owed to foreign bankers. The immediate problem was resolved by arranging for Mexico to receive new loans from other governments (principally the U.S. government) and from international lending agencies (principally the International Monetary Fund—the IMF). Mexico was to use the new loans to pay off the old loans— never mind how it would pay off the new loans; that was a problem for another day.

Beyond the immediate events, however, it soon became apparent that Mexico's problem was a general one. During the 1970s, in many countries of the third world (and also in Eastern Europe), central governments took huge loans from foreign banks. What's more, independent government agencies and private enterprises in these same countries had also taken on foreign debt, with the central governments guaranteeing payment. On top of this, there were substantial additional private obligations which, while not formally guaranteed by the governments, placed further strains on these countries' abilities to pay.

For all of Latin America and the Caribbean, external debt rose some tenfold between 1970 and 1982. (However, since inflation reduced the value of the dollar almost 60 percent in this period, in real terms the region's debt rose only about fourfold.) Total external debt for the region stood at $325.6 billion in 1982, while external public debt—the share owed or formally guaranteed by governments—was $216.1 billion.[1]

Of course, it is not the size of the debt in itself that creates the problem, but the size of the debt *relative to a country's ability to pay.* Since the debt must be repaid in dollars (or a currency readily convertible to dollars), a country's ability to pay depends principally on its earnings from exports. Therefore, a relative measure of the magnitude of the debt is provided by comparing the payments on the debt ("debt servicing") to export earnings. For the four largest debtors in

Table 1
Latin America's Largest Debtors:
Debt and Debt-Service Ratios, 1983–87

	Total external debt in billions of dollars			Debt-service actually paid as a percent of merchandise exports		
	1983	*1985*	*1987*	*1983*	*1985*	*1987*
Argentina	45.1	48.3	51.6	109.3	98.2	(89.6)*
Brazil	93.6	105.1	121.3	58.2	53.1	35.8
Mexico	92.3	96.9	105.1	62.5	57.3	55.0
Venezuela	37.3	34.7	32.5	25.8	19.4	(48.4)*

*These figures are for 1986.
Source: Inter-American Development Bank, *Economic and Social Progress in Latin America: 1988 Report* (Washington, D.C., 1988).

Latin America—Brazil, Mexico, Argentina, and Venezuela, which together account for more than three-quarters of the region's foreign debt—these figures are shown for the mid-1980s in Table 1. Of these four, only Venezuela (with its large oil exports) was using less than half of its export earnings to service its debt in 1983; Argentina, on the other hand, was making payments that exceeded its total export earnings.

As the decade proceeded, Argentina, Brazil, and Mexico were able to lower their debt-service ratios, but this was largely accomplished by taking on more debt and rescheduling payments. New debt was used to pay off old debt, with the new debt having a longer payback period; in this way, the problems were pushed into the future. For Venezuela, with the weakening market for oil, the debt-service ratio rose substantially.

All this debt had been a fine device in the 1970s. The

funds—coming primarily from large banks in New York, Tokyo, London, and Frankfurt—allowed economic growth to continue in much of the third world through a decade when economic slowdown had become the order of the day in most of the advanced capitalist countries. For the third world as a whole—that statistical category called "developing countries"—real gross national product rose at over 5 percent a year during the 1970s, almost as rapidly as during the 1960s. In the twenty-four "advanced" countries that make up the Organization for Economic Cooperation and Development (OECD), output had grown at 5 percent a year in the 1960s, but fell off to hardly more than 3 percent in the 1970s.[2]

The situation could not be sustained, however. The loans that had been taken on by third world governments had to be paid off, as I noted, in dollars or other "hard currency." Hard currencies could only be obtained by exporting to the advanced countries or by taking new loans. The disparity between what had to be paid and what could be earned from exports mounted during the 1970s. Then, with the worldwide and severe recession of the early 1980s, the money simply was not there. In order to meet their obligations, governments used funds that would otherwise have gone to different purposes and instead sent them off to the banks: Funds that would have gone to import food were used to pay the debt. Funds that would have been used for development projects were used to pay the debt. Funds that would have been used to import new machinery and build new factories were used to pay the debt. In short, in order to meet the obligations to foreign bankers, immediate economic well-being and economic growth in much of the third world had to be put aside.

Of course, from a purely technical standpoint, neither economic well-being nor growth *had* to be put aside. If the rich in Latin America, the people who had gained the most from the debt-financed expansion of the preceding years, could have been forced to pay, things would have been very different. From the standpoint of political reality, however, such an option is hardly relevant—that is, it is hardly relevant short of revolution.

Within the context of the current reality, when a country begins to divert huge amounts of resources to pay its debts and economic growth stops, the situation feeds on itself and gets worse and worse. The banks, which had been all too willing to provide funds during the 1970s, now pulled out. New money was available only to pay off old debts, and then only if the IMF was able to assure that the debtor governments would cooperate with "austerity programs"—programs that would continue the policy of diverting funds from consumption and investment to pay off the banks. In addition, the crisis precipitated a massive capital flight from the third world. Wealthy individuals in many countries changed their assets into dollars and placed them safely in U.S. (or Swiss) banks. Capital flight was especially severe in Mexico, where access to U.S. funds was relatively easy. By some estimates, assets held outside the country by Mexican citizens add up to as much as the Mexican foreign debt of $100 billion.[3]

It has become commonplace to say that the countries of the third world cannot pay their debts, and that this inability to pay *is* the crisis. It is more accurate to say that they *can* pay, but only through a major disruption of economic life, a severe curtailment of consumption, and a virtual end to investment. This is a prescription for payment that brings immediate misery and promises more misery in the future. Thus the crisis lies in *this misery itself* and in the political and social disruptions that it portends.

The disruptions have in fact been with the debt crisis from its inception, and ironically they have precipitated some positive changes. Early in the 1980s, economic turmoil made a substantial contribution to the termination of military rule in Brazil, Argentina, Bolivia, and Uruguay. Throughout Latin America, the debt crisis has continued to put severe pressure on established regimes and has given impetus to the political opposition. In Mexico's 1988 presidential election, massive fraud was necessary to maintain the half-century reign of the ruling party. In late 1988 in Brazil, parties of the left won extensive victories in local elections, and socialists became leading contenders for the presidency. In Argentina, in Peru, in Chile, in Ecuador, in Venezuela, partly as a result of the economic disorder engendered by the debt crisis, partly due to the momentum generated by change elsewhere in the region, and partly because of factors particular to each country, progressive oppositional forces made notable gains. For those who sit in the bastions of power and preserve "international order," the debt crisis has been, to say the least, cause for concern.*

The War Against Latin America

Of course the disruptions have not been confined to orderly, formal processes of political change. Periodic, though not frequent, riots in Latin America have been warning signs, revealing the tenuous nature of social peace in the third world. In Brazil, nationwide rioting and looting of su-

---

*As the debt crisis itself extends beyond Latin America, so too does its political and social impact. In the Philippines, for example, the Marcos regime fell, not only because of its own venality, but also as a result of economic disorder connected to its huge foreign debt. In Eastern Europe too, debt difficulties have been an impetus to far-reaching change. However, in some countries—South Korea is the most notable case—a large growth of foreign debt has not been followed, at least as yet, by economic crisis.

permarkets greeted the government's 1983 signing of an IMF austerity agreement. In the Dominican Republic, a 1984 government agreement with the IMF led to rioting that left 184 dead, while hundreds were wounded and some 5,000 were arrested. Most recently, in early 1989, when the Venezuelan government attempted to deal with its debt-generated fiscal difficulties by raising food and public transport prices, riots and a military response left some 250 dead in the streets.

The rising misery and conflict of the debt crisis has induced Brazil's socialist leader, Luis Ignacio Silva ("Lula"), to declare that:

> The third world war has already started—a silent war, not for that reason any less sinister. This war is tearing down Brazil, Latin America, and practically all the third world. Instead of soldiers dying there are children, instead of millions of wounded there are millions of unemployed; instead of destruction of bridges there is the tearing down of factories, schools, hospitals and entire economies. . . . It is a war by the United States against the Latin American continent and the third world. It is a war over the foreign debt, one which has as its main weapon interest, a weapon more deadly than the atom bomb, more shattering than a laser beam.[4]

For a decade, this "war" has been pursued without equivocation by the U.S. government. As though following a take-no-prisoners policy, the Reagan administration rejected any discussion of debt relief. It used the debt crisis to restructure third world economies, to push its agenda of open markets, privatization, and social cutbacks. The Reagan administration had allies in its "war" effort. The IMF was the vanguard unit; the private banks were the combat troops; and the forces of established order in Latin America, the "elite" classes, welcomed the invading armies and embraced the restructuring agenda.

But the policies of the Reagan administration did not have

universal support, either among the governments of the other advanced capitalist countries or among conservative and business interests in the United States. It was not necessary to have sympathetic concern for the impoverished peoples of the third world in order to recognize that the policy of all-out war might be counterproductive. Shortly after the Bush administration took office in 1989, the war policy, or at least the rhetoric, began to change. The Venezuelan "disruptions" appeared to precipitate a new mood, if not new action. U.S. Treasury Secretary Nicholas Brady began to speak of debt relief, efforts to get private banks to write off some of the debt, and government programs to provide guarantees to the U.S. banks. There was even talk of "forgiving" some of the debt.

When the Mexican government reached a new accord with the banks in the middle of 1989, it was immediately hailed by both the U.S. and Mexican governments as a "breakthrough" and a demonstration that Brady's approach was "feasible." In reality, the Mexican accord provided minimal debt relief for Mexico, and may even lead to an increase in the country's obligations. The banks taking part in the agreement had the choice of forgiving some of Mexico's debt, lowering interest rates, or providing new loans. New loans will once again simply push the problems into the future, and the debt and interest rate reductions, which will bring down Mexico's annual payments by 15 percent at most, will be insufficient to pull the economy out of its severe depression. Moreover, few other governments are likely to receive even as favorable treatment as this; the Mexicans have been the most cooperative in complying with the dictates of the banks, the U.S. government, and the IMF.

Although the Mexican agreement demonstrates the limits of the new mood and the new rhetoric on international debt issues, a new mood and a new rhetoric do exist. They reflect a reality that has been part of the debt crisis since its inception. The so-called third world debt crisis is not confined to the third world. It is a crisis of the *entire international economy*, with causes and effects that transcend events in the debtor countries. Moreover, it is part of a much larger crisis of international capitalism.

The riots and military response in Venezuela in early 1989 only underscored the most obvious aspect of the problem. The drastic decline in living standards in Latin America will surely lead, sooner or later, to political conflict and change that cannot be so easily contained. In Venezuela itself, average consumption levels fell more than 20 percent between 1980 and 1987; in Argentina and Mexico, the decline was around 10 percent. Among Latin America's largest debtors, only Brazil saw some slight increase in average consumption in this period, and in the years after 1987 (for which reliable data are not available) trends there seem to have joined those of the other debtors. Moreover, a sharp decline in real wages—in both Mexico and Brazil the buying power of the minimum wage fell by some 40 percent in the 1980 to 1987 period—suggests that the impact of the economic crisis in Latin America has fallen most heavily on the working population.[5] Regardless of their ideological bent and desire to restructure the economies of the third world, neither the U.S. government nor the established powers in Latin America can continue to ignore the political dangers inherent in these sorts of economic changes.

The Impact Spreads

Equally important, the economic effects of the debt crisis have spread outside the third world. With the high degree of interconnection among the world's economies, depression in one set of countries has a far-reaching impact. For example, just prior to the time that the debt crisis became an official event, the Latin American and Caribbean region as a whole had a near balance of international trade—imports slightly exceeded exports in 1978, 1980, and 1981, while exports were slightly more than imports in 1979. After 1981, the region's imports fell off sharply, and it has run a large trade surplus in each subsequent year: exports exceeded imports by more than 50 percent (a trade surplus of around $35 billion) in both 1984 and 1985. The net effect has been a sharp decline in the demand that Latin America and the Caribbean provided for goods from the rest of the world.[6]

From the perspective of the United States, trade with the third world as a whole has been a major component of the ballooning trade deficit in the 1980s. Leaving aside the oil-exporting countries (OPEC), U.S. exports to the third world were slightly greater than imports (a small trade surplus) in 1980 and 1981; by 1987, imports exceeded exports by more than $50 billion (a huge trade deficit). These trade figures translate directly into U.S. employment problems and a general weakness of U.S. industry. They also begin to tell the story of the rapid rise of the United States' own international debt, as we shall see shortly.[7]

More ominous than the disruption of international trade, however, are the problems that have arisen in world financial markets. If a major default were to take place—if, for example, Brazil or Argentina or Mexico were to terminate its debt payments—the result could be a collapse of the international financial system. Funds would then not be available to finance production, and there would be a severe decline of employment and output worldwide.

A financial collapse is, of course, highly unlikely. Even if a major default were to take place, the governments of the rich countries could—and undoubtedly would—provide funds to the banking system and thus offset the impact of the default.

Yet third world debt is only one part of the very large and general expansion of debt that has taken place in the world economy during the last two decades. In the United States, an era of speculation has generated mergers and leveraged buy-outs on a huge scale, leaving many firms with unprecedented debt burdens. In addition, the real estate market has been affected by speculation; both corporations and consumers have increasingly taken loans to finance their normal activities; farmers are heavily in debt; and of course there is the federal government's own greatly expanded debt. In other countries debt has also risen substantially, fueled by the same forces as are at work in the United States. The situation of the third world debtors is thus part of a much larger problem as far as the viability of financial markets is concerned. Yet the third world debt is large and highly concentrated, and the actions of a single government could have an extreme impact.

When the third world debt crisis was first recognized, even the *Wall Street Journal* conjured up the specter of international financial collapse. The *Journal's* concern was not the third world debt as such, but the fragility of the entire international financial system. In the first column on its front page of November 10, 1982, there appeared a fantasy scenario of an international financial panic. The scenario begins on December 2, 1982, with "a small Hong Kong lending company . . . [which] has been aggressively plunging most of its $7 million in borrowed money into Hong Kong real estate." As the real estate market collapses, the lending company closes its doors. The scenario continues as the lending company's banker runs short of funds, and it turns to "the huge $30 billion Eastern Imperial Bank of Hong Kong" to bail it out. But Eastern Imperial finds that its large depositors are getting worried and are taking out their funds, so it turns to international capital markets. Soon the scenario has "huge sums of money . . . [moving] electronically around the world as banks, big investors, multinational companies, and Arab governments shift their dollars to 'safe havens.'" Then, in spite of efforts by the Federal Reserve, banks in the United States start to get into trouble, and, "on December 12, gloom spreads through the world banking community as banks begin to fall like ninepins following the Argentinean government's announcement" that it is repudiating its foreign debt.

The world economy has come a good distance since 1982, and there has been no financial collapse. There have been some major bank failures: the most notable in the United States was that of the Continental Illinois Bank (in 1984), at the time the country's eighth largest commercial bank. There was also the stock market crash of late 1987 and the ongoing debacle of the defaults of savings and loan companies. Moreover, some individual third world governments have held up payments on their debt: Bolivia and Peru were small cases, but for a period in 1987 Brazil publicly delayed its payments and Argentina quietly did not pay during 1988 and 1989. Other governments have declared that they are on the brink of default, with insufficient funds to meet pending obligations.

But each of these moments has passed without collapse, partly because the U.S. government has acted as a "lender of last resort," providing money either directly to the principals, as with several loans to favored Latin American governments and the bailout of the savings and loan companies, or indirectly by a general provision of funds to the banking industry, as in the wake of the stock market crash. Perhaps more important, collapse has been avoided because there has been continual, though slow, economic expansion in the United States and other advanced countries. Yet even with economic expansion, particular firms and particular industries in these countries have developed problems. The saving factor has been that the problems have not appeared everywhere at the same time, and they therefore could be contained. Thus when the government provided funds to limit the extent of the damage, it succeeded.*

But what happens when the next recession comes? Economic collapse in the 1980s was avoided only by measures that increased all types of debt in the international economy, and especially in the United States. When the next recession comes, therefore, governments, firms, and consumers carrying heavy debt loads will be unable to obtain the funds to meet their obligations. Defaults and bankruptcies will be numerous, and the extensive debt connections will spread the impact rapidly and widely. Any recession is therefore likely to become a severe one, and the dangers of financial collapse will be substantial.

Whereas in 1982 total third world debt was $831 billion,

---

*In addition, partly because of pressure from government regulators and partly through their own actions, the large U.S. banks are generally in a stronger financial position than they were in the early 1980s. The case of the largest U.S. bank, Citicorp, is illustrative. In 1982, its loans to Latin America and the Caribbean amounted to 340 percent of its primary capital, which was only $5.5 billion. By 1984, it had raised its primary capital to $8.9 billion, and its loans to Latin America and the Caribbean amounted to 207 percent of primary capital. (The data are from the company's annual reports. "Primary capital" is the difference between a bank's assets and liabilities, and is what the bank has to fall back on if loans fail. When risky loans are large relative to primary capital, depositors may begin to view the bank as a poor place to keep their funds.) By the late 1980s, there was little reason to think that any of the large banks was immediately in danger because of its third world debt alone. Nonetheless, one category of debt is never "alone," and serious problems with third world debt would weaken the banks so that they would be more vulnerable to problems arising from their other loans. Moreover, even with the improvement in their positions, in 1988 the third world debt of the nine largest U.S. money center banks amounted to 91 percent of their primary capital. (On this see Richard E. Feinberg and Gordon H. Hanson, "LDC Debt Will Restructure U.S. Banking," *Challenge* [March/April 1989]).

by 1989 the "solutions" to the debt crisis had increased that figure to $1.3 trillion. As for debt in the United States—where federal government deficits, along with growing corporate and consumer debt, were the fuel for expanding demand throughout the 1980s—the ratio of total debt to GNP rose by nearly a third over the course of the decade. This phenomenon—total debt expanding more rapidly than GNP—is a significant departure from the historical experience in the United States: in each seventeen- to eighteen-year-long cycle between 1897 and 1966, the ratio of net new borrowing to GNP hovered at around 9 percent; between 1967 and 1986, however, this figure rose to 14.6 percent, a 60 percent increase over the historical average.[8]

There is no way to determine in advance when a debt burden will become unsustainable. The debt process is a bit like building a tower with a set of children's blocks. We cannot tell ahead of time how high we can go, how many blocks we can pile on top of each other, but we do know that there is a limit. If we keep going higher and higher, at some point the whole structure will come tumbling down. There are, of course, ways to extend the limit. We can widen the base of the tower, for example, or construct some support structures. There comes a point, however, where we are devoting all our efforts and resources to shoring up the tower.

With the current debt situation, more and more resources are being devoted to "shoring up the tower." The specter of default by various Latin American debtors has brought forth large allocations of credit by the U.S. government, both directly and through the IMF. Such infusions of credit for special problems leave the U.S. monetary authorities—the Federal Reserve System—less flexibility in managing the overall supply of credit. The additional credit contributes to general inflationary pressures and to the persistence of high interest rates, both of which have costly repercussions throughout the economy. Moreover, in extending credit and thus building the tower of debt even higher, the monetary authorities raise the level of uncertainty that exists among people investing in financial markets. Again, the effect is to keep interest rates higher than they would otherwise be. The whole process can be costly, even if the structure never actually tumbles.*

The U.S. Debt

During the 1980s, as I have said, economic growth in the United States was a central factor in preventing a breakdown of the international financial system. That growth was maintained, however, by a set of policies and circumstances that generated a huge foreign debt for the United States.

Throughout most of the twentieth century, into the early 1980s, the United States was the world's principal creditor nation. U.S. holdings of foreign assets—loans and equity investments—exceeded assets held in the United States by foreigners. This "net international investment position" grew to a peak of $141 billion in 1981. The figure declined slightly to $137 billion in 1982 and then began to plummet. By the end of 1988, the net international investment position stood at *minus* $487 billion (see Figure 4.1). Perhaps no

---

*It would be difficult to isolate the different factors that account for the high interest rates of the 1980s, but third world debt is certainly not the largest among them. In any case, it is quite clear that in the 1980s, real interest rates in the United States were substantially higher than in preceding years. (The "real" interest rate is the rate charged by creditors less the rate of inflation.) According to one recent report, real after-tax interest rates on consumer loans fluctuated roughly between 4 and 8 percent in the 1980s, while they had varied roughly between 2 and 4 percent in the 1970s. (See *Business Week*, 17 April 1989, p. 12; also see Figure 4.2.)

other set of data reveals as clearly the extreme instability of U.S. international economic relations in the current period.*

There are many differences between the U.S. foreign debt and the foreign debts of third world nations, not the least of which is that the U.S. debt is payable in the country's own currency. Nonetheless, third world debt and U.S. foreign debt are part of the same story. They have common roots, and they have some common effects.

The third world debt story and the U.S. debt story can both be told as part of the larger tale of the way the U.S. government has responded to stagnation and international instability. In the late 1960s and early 1970s, with the first signs of stagnation and U.S. imperial decline, the U.S. government handled its macroeconomic affairs in a way that laid the foundation for the expansion of international debt generally and the appearance of the third world debt crisis in particular. In the 1980s, still responding to stagnation and also attempting to restore its imperial power, the government initiated a set of macroeconomic policies that generated the U.S. foreign debt. Thus the various parts of the international debt saga tie together, both in their root causes and in the way the U.S. government's economic policies transformed these root causes into the particular problems that confront us now.

In the same way that the debt crisis has led to misery and economic disorder in the third world, the U.S. foreign debt has been part of a larger picture of economic hardship and disruption in this country. Such hardship and disruption have often appeared as a product of the huge shift in U.S. international trade that occurred in the 1980s. U.S. workers

---

*As will be discussed in Chapter 4, the absolute values of these figures are not very reliable. However, the huge relative shift that took place was very real indeed.

have lost jobs as the products they produce have been replaced by imports, and entire communities have felt the impact. Moreover, there has been little expansion of jobs in export industries to balance these losses. Of course, the impact of job loss has gone far beyond the workers immediately affected and far beyond their communities. The threat of "international competition" has been a powerful weapon in the hands of employers in virtually every industry, used to beat back workers' demands for higher wages. We see the result in the stagnation of real wages and in the growing inequality of income distribution in the United States.

But trade imbalances and foreign debt are two sides of the same coin. As I shall show in Chapter 4, in explaining the debt we explain the trade deficit. Either, or both, can be seen, along with the more fundamental problems of stagnation and international instability, as the cause of hardship and disruption.

Furthermore, in the United States as in Latin America, working people—the public in general—are told that they must bear the burden of repaying the foreign debt. Obligations to foreigners must be met, we are told, by a real transfer of resources in the future. To pay off the debt, we will have to export more than we import, and this means less goods and services for domestic use. We are told that sacrifice will be necessary, that the public must pay for the "binge" that brought on the debt. As in the third world, so too in the United States: we are told that we will have to accept an austerity program.

So the stories come together. Third world debt and the U.S. foreign debt are connected parts of a larger phenomenon. By dealing with the two stories as parts of this larger tale, we can learn a good deal about the interactions between national policy and international disorder, about stagnation and instability, about the rules of the game. José Arcadio Buendia might find it a worthwhile contest.

2

U.S. Imperial Decline and the Basis of International Debt

Not so very long ago the U.S. government and businesses based in the United States held a joint position of unchallenged dominance within the capitalist world. In that era, roughly the twenty-five years following World War II, the government built military alliances around the world, extended its diplomatic role in regions where the United States had been a secondary power, and expanded its presence in regions where it was already dominant. The North Atlantic Treaty Organization (NATO) was complemented by regional alliances (the South East Asian Treaty Organization and the Central Treaty Organization), and U.S. military bases were established in virtually every corner of the globe. The U.S. government was able to pressure governments far and near to adopt "correct" policies and to be hospitable to U.S. businesses. Usually, this "pressure" could be exerted successfully through diplomatic channels, behind which U.S. aid-giving programs operated as an effective lever of persuasion. Persuasion, however, always took place against the backdrop of overwhelming U.S. military power, and in several instances the United States exercised its military option—for example, in Greece in 1947, Iran in 1953, Guatemala in 1954, Lebanon in 1958, Cuba in 1961, and the Dominican Republic in 1965, to say nothing of Korea, Vietnam, Berlin, and Quemoy and Matsu.*

As the foundation for its international economic role after World War II, the U.S. government organized the basic institutional structures of the international system. Foremost among these were the monetary arrangements established at the Bretton Woods conference in 1944. Bretton Woods was important because it gave formal certification to the primary role of the United States in the coming postwar order. The most significant aspect of these arrangements was that the governments of the leading capitalist nations agreed to build the postwar international economy around the U.S. dollar. In other words, they agreed that they would buy and sell their own currencies so as to maintain a fixed exchange rate with the dollar. For its part, the U.S. government agreed to exchange dollars for gold at $35 per ounce.

This system of fixed exchange rates and dollar-gold convertability had several consequences. It assured that U.S. businesses would always have funds for their international activities (since dollars would be readily acceptable) and that the value of those dollars would be relatively high (because foreign interests would demand dollars not only to purchase U.S. goods but also to hold as reserves and to use for transactions not involving the United States). Moreover, it assured

---

*This list of examples is far from complete. In the context of examining the controversy over the President's unilateral power to deploy U.S. troops, the *Wall Street Journal* (15 January 1987) provided a list of "137 cases [between 1798 and 1970] where the president sent troops into imminent hostilities or transferred arms or other war material abroad without any congressional authorization." This list includes twenty-one cases between 1946 and 1970, ranging from the Korean war and the build-up of forces in Vietnam to such actions as deploying troops off the coasts of Venezuela (1958) and Haiti (1963) and sending Marines to Indonesia in 1957 and 1958 "to protect U.S. lives and property during . . . revolt[s]." Neither the CIA-conducted interventions in Iran and Guatemala nor the U.S.-sponsored invasion of Cuba in 1961 are part of this list.

that the U.S. government would have the power to force macroeconomic policies on other governments; the United States could act as it saw fit, and other governments, committed to maintaining fixed exchange rates, would have to adjust. (Of course, the stability and maintenance of the system depended upon some restraint by the U.S. government in exercising this power, as we shall see shortly.)

The postwar arrangements also included the organizational structures designed to operate and control the new system. The International Monetary Fund (IMF) would handle problems of short-term stability, providing funds and imposing programs when governments were not able to manage their foreign accounts. The International Bank for Reconstruction and Development (World Bank), buttressed in its activities by various regional banks, would concern itself with long-term economic development. The General Agreement on Tariffs and Trade (GATT) would facilitate the reduction of barriers to trade among nations. In each case, partly through formal voting rights, partly through its provision of a large share of the budget, and partly through its general economic and political power, the U.S. government thoroughly dominated these organizations. Indeed, through the 1980s there seems to have been no public instance of a major policy dispute in which one of these institutions acted in opposition to the United States.

The activity of U.S.-based businesses in the world economy provided the economic power behind the expanding international role of the U.S. government, while that expanding political power was simultaneously a foundation for business expansion. In the postwar period, U.S. firms greatly increased their international operations, extending their control of mineral resources in the third world and setting up production operations in Europe and elsewhere in order to penetrate and control growing markets.

The principal instruments of this expansion were multinational corporations, based in the United States and operating subsidiaries around the globe. In the late nineteenth and early twentieth centuries, as very large firms had come to dominate the economic landscape, as the world economy had become more thoroughly interconnected by modern communications networks, and as workers in many countries had become subject to the common discipline of wage labor systems, multinational firms had appeared as major actors in the international economy. Their full development, however, was held off by the disruption of two world wars and the Great Depression. After 1945 the multinationals—with the U.S.-based firms far in the lead—appeared as the organizers of the new international economic order.

While the rise of multinational firms after World War II was an important long-term development in the history of international capitalism, short-term circumstances also gave a substantial impetus to the role of the U.S.-based firms. With the dollar overvalued because of its role in the new monetary arrangements, U.S. exports were relatively expensive for foreigners while foreign assets were relatively cheap for U.S. firms. Moreover, European governments were bent on restricting imports as a means of fostering the postwar reindustrialization of their economies, and many third world governments were committed to protectionism in order to continue the process of import-substituting industrialization that had begun during the 1930s and war years (particularly in Latin America). As a consequence, if U.S. firms were to have access to growing markets, they would have to invest abroad.

And invest abroad they did. Between 1950 and 1965 the value of the foreign assets of U.S. firms grew at roughly twice the pace of the domestic gross national product. In 1950, the foreign direct holdings of U.S. firms amounted to some $11 billion; by 1965 they stood at $47 billion. In terms of the importance of this foreign investment to profits, foreign earnings as a share of after-tax profits of U.S. nonfinancial corporations rose from 10 percent in 1950 to 22 percent by 1965.*

The largest U.S. industrial firms were central actors in the postwar overseas expansion. In 1950 General Motors, for example, was annually producing less than 200,000 vehicles abroad. By 1952 the figure was approximately 600,000, and in another year, with European production being supplemented by that of Australia and Brazil, GM was producing over 1 million vehicles in its foreign plants. The boom continued into the early part of the next decade: between 1963 and 1964, GM's overseas production grew by a quarter of a million. Accordingly, the profits from foreign investment were highly concentrated in the largest firms. In 1965, thirteen industrial corporations, all among the top twenty-five on the Fortune 500 list, accounted for 41.2 percent of foreign earnings.[1]

The absolute growth of U.S. businesses' foreign holdings in the postwar period was very substantial, but it is even more impressive when viewed in terms of the gains of U.S. firms relative to their foreign rivals. In particular, in Latin America just prior to World War I, only 18 percent of foreign private equity and less than 5 percent of public debt was held by U.S. interests. British interests held 47 percent of foreign private

---

*This rise in the importance of foreign-source profits is all the more significant because it took place during an era of a general rise in the rate of profit in the United States. There are, however, many problems in calculating these figures, and, while the basic nature of the change is clear, not too much significance should be attached to the particular numbers. The asset value figures are from various issues of the U.S. Department of Commerce, *Survey of Current Business;* usually the data are published in the July or August edition. The figures on foreign earnings as a percentage of after-tax corporate profits are from Table XLI in Harry Magdoff, *The Age of Imperialism* (New York: Monthly Review Press, 1969), p. 183.

equity and 70 percent of public debt. In the early 1950s, new direct investment in Latin America from sources other than the United States was negligible, and in the 1960s U.S. interests still accounted for roughly 70 percent of new foreign direct investment. As to the foreign public debt—a matter I will turn to shortly—the United States was supplying about 70 percent in the early 1950s and more than 50 percent even in the early 1960s.[2]

In this era, U.S. international dominance was, of course, limited in the political realm by the Soviet Union, and socialist and nationalist movements throughout the world did not readily accept the economic power of U.S. business. Yet within the wide realm of capitalism—what the U.S. authorities have dubbed the "Free World"—there was no appreciable challenge. Other governments accepted their subordinate position, and businesses based in other nations found ways to fit into an economic milieu organized by U.S. firms.

Hegemony and Stability

The period is often referred to as the era of U.S. hegemony. In modern times, it found its parallel in the degree of dominance exercised by Britain during the middle of the nineteenth century. That had been the era of Pax Britannica, and the post-World War II years became the era of Pax Americana. In each of these periods, a central power generally set the rules for international affairs. Direct political control in the form of colonies was not the principal method of organization in either era. Instead, power flowed from unrivaled economic strength and was backed by seemingly unchallengeable military superiority. In a world of formally independent nations, imperial power nonetheless was the main organizing instrument of international affairs.*

There is a good deal of argument about whether the imperial power of Pax Americana was a beneficent or malevolent force in international affairs. There is, however, no argument over the existence of that power or over its importance as the organizing foundation for international economic affairs. The great strength of the U.S. government and business in the international system provided one of the central pillars of the very rapid economic advance of the capitalist nations during the quarter century following World War II. Stable financial arrangements, few inhibitions on the movement of investment funds, and a relatively open organization of trade resulted in the rapid growth of international commerce, a more thorough international integration of capitalist economies. The flow of goods, capital, and technology across international boundaries proved to be a strong stimulus to economic growth.

As it turned out, however, U.S. hegemony was ephemeral. The success of the era meant the restrengthening of the economies of Japan and Europe. Both U.S. government aid and investment by U.S. firms had been necessary to rebuild

---

*Britain did directly control its colonies, but it did not acquire them during its period of hegemony, which we could date from the end of the Napoleonic Wars in 1815 until into the last quarter of the century. In this period, the British role in Latin America provides a particularly good illustration of hegemonic operations. Britain's extreme military—particularly naval—power and its great industrial strength allowed it to dominate the economies of Latin American countries without incurring the costs of direct colonial control. In various instances, British action was decisive in determining the outcome of political conflicts in the region, and British support always went to those who maintained free trade, providing both markets and raw materials for "the workshop of the world." As British power was challenged by other nations toward the end of the century, there was a new rush for colonies, exemplified by the dividing up of Africa after the Berlin Conference of 1884–85.

the international economy and to establish the very profitable international expansion of the U.S. firms. Yet this great imperial success also reestablished alternative centers of growth. Businesses based in Japan and Europe came to challenge U.S. firms in every corner of the globe, including in the United States itself.

The changes were developing in the 1960s and became clear in the 1970s. Between 1967 and 1978, while U.S.-based multinationals continued to expand in absolute terms, they saw their share of total foreign investment erode from 50 percent to 45 percent (not a large change, perhaps, but a dramatic shift from the trend of the 1950s and 1960s). In the same decade, the combined share of foreign direct investment held by West German and Japanese firms leaped from 4.6 percent to 14.7 percent.[3] In terms of the relative position of U.S. firms in the world market generally—as opposed to simply foreign investment—the changes have been summed up as follows:

> In 1959, an American company was the largest in the world in 11 of 13 major industries into which manufacturing plus commercial banking can be grouped. . . . By 1976 the U.S. was leading in 7 of 13. . . . The number of U.S. companies among the world's top 12 declined in *all* industry groups except aerospace between 1959 and 1976. . . . Although the U.S. still had 68 or 44% of the 156 largest companies in the 13 industry groups in 1976, it was down from 111 (or 71%) in 1959.[4]

These changes in relative industrial strength had their counterpart in a growing independence of economic policy. Ironically, in the early 1970s, as the increasing connections among advanced capitalist economies made the coordination of policy among governments seem most essential, the basis for that coordination slipped away. U.S. Secretary of State Henry Kissinger lamented to *Business Week* (13 January 1975) at the beginning of 1975: "One interesting feature of our recent discussions with both the Europeans and Japanese has been the emphasis on the need for economic coordination. . . . How you, in fact, coordinate policies is yet an unresolved problem." The policy coordination problem had become especially severe in the face of OPEC's oil price increases. At a 1974 conference where the United States attempted to establish some cohesion among the oil-consuming nations, "Kissinger's entire argument was couched in terms of 'interdependence,' suggesting that nations which sought to promote their self-interest at the expense of others would wind up injuring themselves—by weakening the entire world system of production, trade, and investment for decades to come." The lack of U.S. success at the conference was shown by the response of the French: "For its part, France has followed the ancient doctrine of 'sauve qui peut'— or roughly, 'every man for himself'" (*New York Times*, 13 February 1974).

The end of U.S. hegemony, however, was brought about by more than the challenge from the other advanced capitalist countries. In the late 1960s and early 1970s the United States faced a severe challenge to its relationship with the third world. Here too success generated failure. As the success of U.S. hegemony had required support for the reemergence of rivals to Japan in Europe, so did it require the continual extension and protection of capitalism in the periphery of the system.

As I have noted, during the postwar era the U.S. government acted on numerous occasions to apply pressure through military action. Yet in the late 1960s and early 1970s, the U.S. government found itself extended beyond its capabilities when it attempted to play policeman for the operations of international capitalism. Unable to win the war in Vietnam or to obtain popular support for its effort at home, the government was forced to pursue inflationary policies that undermined the strength of the economy. Then, as the economy weakened, the government was less able to pursue a successful military policy in Vietnam. As I shall explain shortly, the macroeconomic policies the government followed in connection with the war had a severe impact on the stability of the international financial system. Those policies led directly to the termination of the Bretton Woods arrangements; it was at this point that it was widely recognized that the international organization of power had changed.

No one doubts that the United States remains the leading power among capitalist nations, but the joint ability of U.S. government and business to set the rules of international affairs no longer exists. The U.S. government cannot readily impose economic policies on its allies. U.S. business is no longer unchallenged—quite the contrary. It has had to adjust to challenges from Japan and Europe, from rising economic powers such as Korea and Brazil, and from the OPEC nations. Even in the realm of conflict with the Soviet Union, the United States is facing increasing dissension among its allies.

The decline of U.S. hegemony is reflected in the poorer economic performance of the capitalist nations during the period since the early 1970s. It is also reflected in a higher degree of instability in international economic affairs. Of course, the change of international power relations was not the only factor that led to the appearance of relative stagnation and instability in the advanced capitalist economies. Several other special factors had propelled the system upward in the postwar decades. Among these were: the huge demand for investments to reconstruct war-devastated economies, the rapid escalation of military spending as the cold war developed, the technological spin-offs from the war and subsequent military spending, and an upsurge of demand stimulated by the spread of the mass use of automobiles. But by the 1970s the force of these special factors had waned.

Moreover, the effective operation of all these factors had depended on a considerable degree of international stability, and that stability was provided by U.S. hegemony. Thus when U.S. hegemony came to an end, a crisis developed for the entire system. It was a general crisis in the sense that the bases for the system's success had broken down, and some great changes would have to take place, some new modes of international organization and production established, before another era of success could begin.*

Foundations of International Debt Expansion

As U.S. power began to ebb in the 1960s and as U.S. hegemony came to a marked termination in the early 1970s with the demise of the Bretton Woods monetary arrangements, a sequence of events was set in motion that led to a new role for banking and debt in the international economy. A defining feature of U.S. hegemony had been the central role

---

*The onset of relative stagnation and instability in the world economy involved more than the decline of U.S. hegemony and the weakening of the "special factors" I have noted here. These changes were, for example, bound together with a disruption of capital-labor relations and a decline in the capacity of governments to regulate national economies. However we organize our explanation of events, it is clear that the very rapid and stable expansion of capitalist economies in the postwar quarter century resulted from some special circumstances. The much slower growth and instability of subsequent decades might be viewed as more "normal." Two views that, although in some ways differing, support this general line of argument can be found in Harry Magdoff and Paul Sweezy, *Stagnation and the Financial Explosion* (New York: Monthly Review Press, 1987), and Samuel Bowles, David M. Gordon, and Thomas E. Weisskopf, *Beyond the Wasteland: A Democratic Alternative to Economic Decline* (Garden City, N.Y.: Anchor Press/Doubleday, 1983).

of the dollar in international commerce. With dollars used for trade among other nations and held as reserves by other governments, large dollar holdings grew up overseas. These holdings reflected the fact that U.S. businesses, the government, and private individuals were purchasing more abroad than foreign interests were purchasing from the United States. (This is analogous to a private individual being able to write checks on her or his bank account and to operate as though many of those checks will never be cashed in.)

In the short run this was a very advantageous arrangement for the United States. In the longer run, however, the situation presented a problem for both the United States and for the general stability of the international economy. As the holdings of dollars overseas grew—and they grew at a rate of roughly $2 billion per year during the 1960s—the structure of the monetary system became increasingly unstable.[5] (From today's perspective, an increment of $2 billion per year to the foreign holdings of dollars seems like a paltry sum. However, at the end of the 1960s, foreign dollar and Eurodollar reserves were still only $20 billion, and an increase of $2 billion per year was therefore considerable.)

The dollar's role had been secure as long as foreign interests maintained confidence that the U.S. government could redeem their dollar holdings, but, as those holdings grew, it became evident that the U.S. government could not back the entire system with gold. It was not at all clear how far the system could be pushed, but considerable concern developed among international investors in the late 1960s. Their fear was that as the supply of dollars continued to rise as a result of growing U.S. spending abroad, the demand for dollars would continue to lag behind, and ultimately the value of the dollar would have to fall relative to other currencies. Those holding dollars would then suffer losses. Moreover, the very existence of such a concern could cause the value of the dollar to fall, as speculators shifted their holdings to other currencies. If this process were to commence, the whole international economy could be disrupted and all the players in the game would suffer.

In the late 1960s, the U.S. government took advantage of the dollar-dependent international financial system as domestic and international conflicts placed severe fiscal strains on the government and threatened to disrupt the U.S. economy. In order simultaneously to finance the war in Indochina and buy racial and social harmony in urban centers, the government followed a deficit spending program financed through an expansion of the supply of dollars.

While one might expect the expansion of the money supply to have led to considerable inflation, in fact price increases were relatively mild in the United States during the late 1960s. The structure of international monetary arrangements allowed U.S. inflation to be exported. As the U.S. government ran deficits and increased the money supply, more and more dollars found their way overseas; in fact, the normal spending of funds, which would have spread the dollars abroad, was enhanced in this period by the growth of military spending. In these circumstances, central banks in other nations were faced with a dilemma. They could, on the one hand, refuse to increase the supply of their own currencies to the extent necessary to buy up the extra dollars. Such action, however, would tend to exacerbate the already existing downward pressure on the value of the dollar and threaten to disrupt the functioning of the international economy. On the other hand, they could expand the supplies of their own currencies to buy up the dollars. This latter course of action, however, would increase inflation in their own economies. In general, foreign central bankers accepted their secondary role, took the dollars, and imported the U.S.-government-created inflation into their own economies. (The acquiescence of European bankers was made easier by the fact that inflation was not a paramount problem for them in the 1960s.)

It was a process that could not last. During 1970, the recession in the United States led the government to push down interest rates in an effort to stimulate investment and growth. The principal result, however, was that the lower interest rates led investors to move large amounts of short-term assets (investments in securities) out of the United States. Selling their holdings of dollars in favor of other currencies, international investors were placing severe downward pressure on the value of the dollar. As the process continued into the first half of 1971, it became clear that the situation could no longer be sustained. The U.S. government then eliminated the convertability of dollars for gold and placed a 10 percent surcharge on imports, effectively devaluing the dollar and drastically altering international monetary arrangements. Thoroughly crippled by these events, the Bretton Woods system was formally terminated in 1973.

Nonetheless, the U.S. government's efforts to preserve empire and prolong domestic economic expansion had already initiated a surge in the international supply of money, a wave of growth in international liquidity. This general growth in the supply of funds and, in particular, the growth in the supply of dollars held abroad were the foundation for the growth of international lending that would occur in the subsequent decade.

The dollars held abroad by commercial banks came to be called "Eurodollars," and the whole new wave of lending associated with the growth of international liquidity came to be called the "Eurocurrency Market." The essential feature that accounts for the rising role of the Eurocurrency Market is its relative lack of regulation. Within the United States the government can and does control the amount of new loans that a bank can finance with every new dollar of deposits; by requiring that banks hold a certain percentage of all deposits in reserve, the government both places a limit on the expansion of loan activity and protects the banking system from putting itself in a position where it cannot meet the demands of depositors for their funds. Moreover, government regulators establish restrictions that limit the degree of risk that can be undertaken by banks in extending new loans.

In the Eurocurrency Market such regulation is virtually absent, and competition among banks tends to push them into riskier and riskier loans and toward holding a smaller and smaller percentage of deposits as reserves. Furthermore, with the operation of the unregulated Eurocurrency Market, individual governments have much less control over the supply of their currencies. When, for example, banks holding dollars abroad loan out those dollars they create new dollars, that is, new claims on goods and services in the United States. Dollars can be lent, and then, when the borrower deposits the new funds back in the banking system, they can be re-lent, and so on and on, the process being limited only by each bank's willingness to take on risk.*

While the Eurocurrency Market came into being during the 1960s as a consequence of the structure of the international monetary system and of the particular policies fol-

---

*Of course, even in the absence of regulation, banks will hold some reserves—i.e., keep some of their money available in order to meet the demands of creditors (depositors). However, there is a cost in holding reserves because they do not earn interest—or at least they earn less interest than funds in use. Moreover, the cost of holding reserves rises as interest rates go up (as they did in the 1970s). By way of illustration, assuming that no interest is paid on reserves, R. M. Pecchioli shows that if the actual reserve requirement is 10 percent, and a bank avoiding regulation can get by holding reserves of 8 percent, then this amounts to a cost advantage of one-fourth of a cent on the dollar when the interest rate is 10 percent. Were the interest rate to double, so too would the cost advantage of holding lower reserves; see *The Internationalization of Banking: Policy Issues* (Paris: OECD, 1983), p. 57.

lowed by the U.S. government, during the 1970s it expanded much farther. Again, U.S. government policies were the prime factor (though the unregulated international banking system, operating as noted above, also played a major role). As the general crisis emerged and slow growth beset the international economy, the government chose to deal with its problems by running large deficits financed through an expansion of the money supply. This policy emerged sharply in 1971 and 1972, and continued to one degree or another throughout the decade.*

In spite of the changes that took place in the international monetary system in the early 1970s, the growing supply of dollars continued to move overseas. U.S. hegemony had come to an end, but the great political and economic power of the United States continued to be reflected in a central, though altered, role for the dollar in international affairs. The Eurocurrency Market, now fully operative, proved an attractive home for surplus dollars. Between the end of 1969 and the end of 1972, foreign dollar claims on the U.S. government and on foreign branches of U.S. banks doubled, and then doubled again by the end of 1977. Similarly, international dollar reserves quadrupled between the end of 1969 and the end of 1972, and then more than doubled again by the end of 1977.[6]

Part of the growth in the amount of funds held in the Eurocurrency Market was due to the arrival of "Petrodollars."

---

*In fiscal years 1971 and 1972 the federal budget deficits were $23 billion and $23.4 billion respectively. With the exception of the $25.2 billion deficit at the peak of the Vietnam War in 1968, these were by far the largest deficits of the post-World War II period. These deficits were to be dwarfed, however, by those of the second half of the 1970s; from 1975 through 1980, the deficit averaged over $60 billion. The principal measure of the money supply, M1, rose by 87 percent in the 1970s, compared to 53 percent in the 1960s, with 1977–78 being the two-year period with most rapid growth (17.1 percent), followed by 1971–72 (16.4 percent). These data are from *The Economic Report of the President, 1985*, pp. 303 and 318.

The rise of oil revenues accruing to OPEC member governments after 1973 was so rapid and so large that in many
countries the funds were not spent as rapidly as they were
obtained (in spite of the huge growth of luxury consumption
by elites and the surge in armaments spending). Surplus
funds were primarily invested in the Eurocurrency Market,
where they served once again to enhance the already expanding credit base. The data noted above, however, make it clear
that the expansion of international liquidity was well established prior to the "energy crisis" of 1973. Furthermore,
during the 1970s two surges of growth in the international
supply of money can be identified, the first during the 1971–
72 period and the later during 1977–78. Each came just
before, rather than after, a major rise in oil prices.[7]

Therefore, although many commentators have attributed
the development of international financial instability to the
Petrodollar phenomenon, the origin of the great expansion of
international liquidity does not lie with the expansion of
OPEC revenues. Moreover, insofar as OPEC surpluses were
important in generating the debt crisis—and they surely
played an important exacerbating if not originating role—
they, like the original emergence of Eurodollars, are best
explained as a symptom of the decline and breakup of U.S.
hegemony. What clearer sign of the ebb of U.S. power than
the ability of a group of peripheral states to alter the organization of international energy markets?

We can thus trace the expansion of international liquidity
to the emergence of a general crisis in two senses. First, the
emergence of the Eurocurrency Market, in both its Eurodollar and Petrodollar components, and the initiation of
liquidity expansion were tied to the crisis as consequences of
the decline of U.S. hegemony. Second, as the crisis evolved
and relative stagnation set in, U.S. government deficits and
monetary expansion continued to fuel the fires of international inflation and liquidity expansion.

The Internationalization of U.S. Banking

Events in the 1970s led to great changes in the practices of U.S. banks. Building on the emergence of the Eurocurrency Market, they became increasingly important and highly competitive actors in the world economy. Slow growth in the advanced capitalist economies, however, limited the market for their funds. As the 1970s progressed, they moved more and more to "push" their funds into the third world. In this process, we see one side of the development of what became the third world debt crisis.

U.S. banks had not participated as much as one might expect in the early post-World War II expansion of U.S. business abroad and until the mid-1960s their foreign operations grew relatively slowly. The growth of the U.S. economy and the more rapid growth of U.S.-based multinationals, which the banks could service from their domestic base, seem to have provided sufficient outlets for bank funds. In the 1960s, however, U.S. banks began to go abroad to join in earning profits from unregulated Eurocurrency operations. Moreover, the U.S. banks were forced to go abroad simply to protect themselves. The general reemergence of the competitive strength of the Japanese and European economies was given extra impetus in the international banking industry by the emergence of the Eurocurrency system. Without well-established foreign operations, U.S. banks would lose some of the foreign business of their U.S.-based customers to foreign rivals; this in turn might give foreign banks an inroad to the U.S. banking market.[8] (In addition, early concern with emerging balance of payments problems in the late 1960s led the U.S. government to establish restrictions, albeit weak ones, on the export of capital. The U.S. banks would have had difficulty, therefore, continuing to service foreign businesses so predominantly from their domestic base.)

Various sets of data show the impressive growth of U.S.-based international banking, beginning in the late 1960s and continuing on through the 1970s and into the 1980s. For example, in 1960 domestic assets accounted for 98.6 percent of U.S. commercial bank assets; by 1967, the figure had fallen, but only to 96.5 percent; in 1980, however, domestic assets had dropped to 74.1 percent.[9] Or, in the Commerce Department's summary of "U.S. International Transactions," consider the category "Receipts of income on U.S. assets abroad," other than income from direct investments and U.S. government receipts. This category is mostly made up of the banks' interest receipts on their foreign loans. In 1960 such receipts stood at $646 million; by 1970 they had grown to $2.7 billion. The figure leaped to $32.8 billion in 1980 and to $59.5 billion in 1984 (see Table 2).

During the 1970s, Citibank's especially aggressive international operations played a major role in making it the largest U.S. bank by the end of the decade. In one year, 1977, 82.2 percent of Citibank's earnings came from international operations. While that figure is an extreme one, composite figures for the ten largest U.S. banks in the years leading up to the recognition of the debt crisis reveal a striking reliance on foreign-source earnings: in the six years 1977 through 1982, those banks obtained 48 percent of their earnings from international operations.[10]

This growth of U.S.-based international banking involved a major shift in the way U.S. capital was involved in the international economy, for it was accompanied by a decline in the rate of growth of U.S. foreign direct investment. During the 1950s and early 1960s, the total value of U.S. foreign direct investment, measured in real terms, increased at a rate of between 7 and 8 percent a year. During the late 1960s and throughout the 1970s, the rate of increase was between 4 and 5 percent, and in the early 1980s the real value of the

Table 2
Receipts of Income on U.S. Assets Abroad, 1960–87
(millions of dollars)

| | *Receipts from:* | | |
	Direct investment (1)	*Other investments* (2)*	*(2) as a % of (1)*
1960	3,621	646	17.8
1965	5,506	1,421	25.8
1970	8,169	2,671	32.7
1975	16,595	7,644	46.1
1980	37,146	32,798	88.3
1981	32,549	50,182	154.2
1982	21,381	58,050	271.5
1983	20,499	51,920	253.3
1984	21,217	59,464	280.3
1985	32,665	50,131	153.2
1986	36,697	45,191	123.1
1987	52,308	46,116	88.2

*Includes primarily interest on bank loans, but also includes returns on other private investments, e.g., on foreign bonds held directly by private individuals.

Note: Returns on direct investments are profits, while receipts on other investments are gross figures.

Source: U.S. Department of Commerce, *Survey of Current Business,* June 1987 and September 1988.

stock of U.S. foreign direct investment declined somewhat.[11]* The dramatic change in the relative importance of foreign direct investment and loans shows up in Table 2, which provides data on the various forms of "Receipts of

---

*The slowdown in the rate of expansion of U.S. foreign direct investment is often missed because the data are not corrected for inflation. If this is not done, the rate of expansion appears quite stable over the entire 1950–80 period. However, since inflation increased fairly steadily from 1965 to 1980, stable expansion in current dollars must mean slowing expansion in real (or constant) dollars.

Income on U.S. Assets Abroad." While receipts from "other investments" (mainly loans) amounted to only 17.8 percent of receipts from direct investment in 1960 and 25.8 percent in 1965, the figure had jumped to 46.1 percent in 1975, before shooting up to the point where receipts from "other investments" greatly exceeded receipts from foreign direct investment in the early 1980s.*

The growth of international banking and the expansion of the Eurocurrency Market generated a new era of competition among U.S. banks. With the greatly increased base from which to make unregulated loans, the banks began to scramble to find new borrowers. Describing his bank's operating procedures during its rapid growth in the 1970s, Citibank Vice-chairman Thomas Theobald told *Business Week* (16 May 1983): ". . . if there [is] an opportunity , take advantage. Don't analyze it to death. . . . Anytime you can get a license, take it; almost anytime you can get a customer relationship with a desired customer, take it."

At a much lower level in the banking hierarchy, S. C. Gwynne described his role as a loan officer in a "medium-sized Midwestern bank with $5 billion in assets." According to Gwynne, who in the late 1970s was "selling money door to door" in the third world: "As a domestic credit analyst, I was taught to develop reasonable asset security for all loans. . . . As an international loan officer, I was taught to forget about

---

*Of course, part of the extreme change in the early 1980s was a result of the appreciation of the dollar. Direct investment yields returns in local currencies which must be transformed—either actually or for accounting purposes—into dollars, while loans are generally denominated in dollars. Conversely, the reversal of the trend in 1985 is partly explained by the depreciation of the dollar. Also, as suggested in the note to Table 2, the two categories of receipts are somewhat different, since returns on direct investment are profits while receipts on other investments are gross interest payments. My point, however, does not depend on comparing the absolute size of the figures in the two series, but on comparing their relative movement over time.

that, and instead to develop a set of rationales that would make the home office feel good about the loan, even though, technically, it was 'unsecured.' "[12]

The new "style" in the banking industry—the shift in psychology away from that of the stodgy, conservative and cautious banker—was rooted in increasing competition. The new level of competition was, in turn, the direct consequence of two objective factors. One of these was the lack of regulation in international finance. Whatever else it accomplishes, regulation of the banking industry serves to limit competition. One bank cannot challenge others by extending its loans on a lesser and more risky reserve base; nor can it take on loans without proper security or extend credit to inherently risky customers. Thus regulation protects banks from combat with one another and from the risks that come with overextension. Yet these constraints did not exist in the Eurocurrency Market.

The second factor that encouraged competition among the banks was the impact of the general economic crisis itself on the demand for funds. With a decline in the growth rates of output and investment within the economies of the advanced capitalist nations, the rate of expansion of profitable and secure loan opportunities also declined. The growth of national output in the advanced countries was substantially less in the 1970s than in the 1960s: in the United States the growth rate of GNP was roughly 3.8 percent in the early period and fell to below 3 percent in the 1970s; for the advanced countries as a whole—using data for the twenty-four countries that make up the Organization for Economic Cooperation and Development (OECD)—growth declined from about 5 percent to a little over 3 percent. The demand for credit, however, is more directly affected by the level of investment than the level of national income. Here the comparison between the 1970s and 1960s is even more striking. In the United States the annual growth rate of gross investment fell from 5.3 percent in the 1960s to 2.8 percent in the 1970s; in Japan, the fall was from 15.3 percent to 3 percent, and in West Germany from 3.9 percent to 1.2 percent.[13]* Thus the onset of the general crisis was characterized by both a great expansion in the supply of loanable funds and a slowdown in the growth of demand for these funds. The banks were then forced to compete increasingly with one another in the search for new customers.

The growing competition for third world customers during the 1970s is revealed by the terms on which loans were made. Data on non-OPEC "Less-developed Countries" show that in the fourth quarter of 1975, the "spread" (the difference between the London Interbank Borrowing Rate and what banks charge their customers) averaged 1.65 percentage points, while the average maturity of loans was about 5.5 years. By the fourth quarter of 1979, the "spread" had fallen to 0.76 percentage points and average maturity had risen to slightly over 10 years.[14] Since there is little reason to think that this improvement reflected an improvement in the economic outlook in the countries receiving the loans, these data are evidence of the growing competition among the banks and of the "loan-pushing" that resulted.

During the 1970s, then, as the general disarray and instability of the advanced capitalist economies began to be

---

*The experience of the 1980s demonstrated that stagnation does not necessarily lead to a decline in the demand for credit. Even slower rates of growth in the 1980s as compared to the 1970s have been associated with a veritable explosion of credit demand in the United States, as noted in Chapter 1. I do not wish to argue here that the onset of stagnation *had* to result in loan-pushing to the third world, but simply that the development of this outlet for funds was encouraged by the slowdown in the advanced countries. Conditions in the 1970s called for a new outlet to be found, and third world countries provided that outlet. When, after 1982, third world governments and businesses were no longer viewed as favored customers, the banks developed new devices and new outlets in the advanced countries themselves.

widely apparent, the factors that provided a basis for the debt crisis of the 1980s had been well established: the rising surge of liquidity, of a large supply of credit, in the international economy; the operation of a relatively unregulated international financial system; the full-scale entrance of the U.S. banks into international markets; rising competition in international banking; and slow economic growth in the advanced capitalist nations. These factors combined to "push" funds out of the central capitalist economies and into the periphery.

3

Dependence and Inequality: The Roots of Latin American Debt

An economic crisis is a period of change, a historic turning point. Old institutions that structured economic relations no longer function, severe disruptions of production and exchange occur, and social conflicts become intense. In such circumstances, there are ever present dangers of political reaction and retrogression, but there are also opportunities for progressive change. In the underdeveloped world—plagued as it is by instability, dependency, and inequality—economic crises are not rare. Indeed, one might go so far as to assert that the condition of underdevelopment is a condition of perpetually recurring crises. Accordingly, among the underdeveloped nations we see centers of both reaction and revolutionary progress.

The current crisis in Latin America, however, is not simply one more in the string of crises that characterizes underdevelopment. It is different because it is part of the broader international crisis that has beset both the center and periphery of the capitalist world—and perhaps also the noncapitalist world—for much of the last two decades. Crises that affect the international economy on such a wide scale appear periodically, perhaps every forty or fifty years. The last such crisis was that which centered around the Great Depression of the 1930s and found its resolution only in the cataclysm of World War II.

Nonetheless, while the current crisis is not confined to Latin America, Latin America is a focal point of considerable importance. As in the early colonial period, when the huge flow of precious metals out of Latin America altered economic relations around the world, events in Latin America today are having repercussions throughout the international economy. Also as in that earlier era, the central events concern the international financial system. The issue then was money in that most basic form of gold and silver. Today it is money in that most abstract form of credit that is the disruptive link between Latin America and the centers of wealth and power.

Latin America's current "debt crisis" of course goes far beyond financial matters, disrupting production and employment on a wide scale. It provides one more illustration of the way the region's destiny is dominated and perverted by its subordination in the international economy. Thus, an examination of the origins and emergence of the crisis in Latin America offers a good opportunity to reanalyze the dynamic of underdevelopment.

The Duality of Dependence and Inequality

During the 1970s, as I explained in the previous chapter, the appearance of a general economic crisis set the stage for the debt crisis. Economic instability and stagnation led to government policies—in particular the expansionist fiscal and monetary policies of the U.S. government—which spawned a great increase of available funds (liquidity) in an essentially unregulated international banking system. Yet instability and stagnation also meant that in the advanced capitalist countries the demand for credit did not keep pace with the burgeoning supply of funds. Faced with a rapid expansion of liquidity that could not be absorbed in the center, the banks began to push funds out into the periphery of world capitalism.

This "push" which contributed to the current financial crisis was complemented by a "pull," a strong demand for credit in the economies of the periphery, especially those in Latin America. In attempting to interpret underdevelopment and determine directions of change in Latin America, this "pull" is of central concern.

It is not an exaggeration to say that the roots of this "pull"—and thus the roots of Latin America's current debt problem—can be traced to the early colonial era, to the way Spanish and Portuguese America were connected to the international economy and to the types of social structures that were established then. During the sixteenth century, economic life in the Spanish colonies was thoroughly dominated by gold and silver. After the original plundering of the Aztec and Inca empires, silver mining, centered in the mountains of Peru, Bolivia, and Mexico, largely defined both social relations in the colonies and the colonies' relation to the rest of the world. The economy of the mines was driven by the European demand for silver, and the rhythm of life in the colonies was subordinate to, and dependent upon, developments in the external world. In addition, the economy of the mines generated a highly unequal, bipolar social structure, with a small group of Spanish and creoles at the top, a large group of indigenous peoples drafted into labor at the bottom, and relatively few others in between.

These two characteristics of the early era—external orientation of economic life and great inequality—have continued to exist in Latin American economies, to one degree or another, down to the current period. In Brazil, where sugar instead of silver was the focus of sixteenth-century production and where African slaves instead of drafted Amerindians did the work, similar conditions prevailed. Dramatic changes have taken place to be sure. Today, Brazil and Mexico are major industrial powers, and mining and agriculture have dwindled to secondary importance. Yet today's industry, and indeed each form of economic activity that has come and gone in Latin America during the last four centuries, has built upon and not transformed (or only minimally transformed) the original external dependence and inequality.

The duality of dependence and inequality that characterizes Latin American history has bred a continuing reliance on an inflow of capital from the center. At any given point of time, a considerable share of the economic surplus generated in Latin America is obligated to pay—through expatriated profits or interest payments—for capital that came from the center in the past. Therefore, the share of the surplus that can be directed toward expansion within the Latin American nations is limited. If growth is to be attained *and* obligations met, then the only option is to take on more direct investment or loans from the center.

In the early colonial era, the foreign extraction of resources from Latin America was blatant, as Spain established a monopoly trade system that assured a highly unequal relation between the "mother country" and its American possessions. According to Celso Furtado, during the sixteenth century, "the value of imports covered only a small fraction of the exports [from the colonies]. The averages over long periods indicate that the value of the precious metals shipped by the private sector was about four times that of total imports."[1]

Throughout the nineteenth century, free trade and British industrial power assured an international division of labor that shifted resources from the Latin American periphery to the world's manufacturing centers. Producing and exporting agricultural goods and minerals, the Latin American nations had little power to determine prices or to appropriate benefits from the nineteenth century's rapid technological advances. The experience is summed up by Stanley Stein and Barbara Stein:

> Massive imports of British manufactures simply crushed local industry based on primitive technology. Inevitably, like the southern United States, Latin America was drawn to search for export staples, traditional or new, to pay for imports. It was drawn to the land and to external sources of dynamism.[2]

Moreover, without an industrial base of its own to generate funds, Latin America further relied on the British to finance and control the railways, banking, and much of the region's commerce.

In the modern era leading into the debt crisis, the same pattern has prevailed. During the decade 1968 to 1979, for Latin America as a whole, the net outflow of dividends and interest amounted to $70.6 billion. (As a basis for comparison, total merchandise imports to the region in 1979 amounted to $70.9 billion.) As a result, the region had a substantial balance of payments deficit on current account which could only be balanced by an inflow of new investment, primarily bank loans.* Of course, the situation varied from country to country and the need for foreign funds became even greater after the oil price increases in 1973 (when the region's trade balance, which had been slightly positive,

---

*A country or region's "balance of payments on current account" is the funds it receives for exports of goods and services less its payments for imports of goods and services. The "services" of capital are included in services, and thus the outflow of profits and interest are treated as payments for imports of services. For a country or region, as for an individual, if imports (purchases) are more than exports (sales), the difference must be made up by taking on liabilities or reducing assets. The adjustment of liabilities and assets appears in the capital account. For a country or region with imports greater than exports, the capital account adjustment can involve borrowing, new foreign direct investment, or a depletion of reserves.

worsened sharply). Yet the continuation of historic patterns in the contemporary period is clear.[3]

Latin America's lack of foreign investment has not, however, simply been a lack of foreign funds. Indeed, as has been widely recognized, in the modern era foreign direct investors—the multinational firms—operating in Latin America often obtain a significant portion of the funds they invest from local capital markets. For example, in the late 1950s and early 1960s a quarter of the funds invested in Latin America by U.S.-based multinational firms came from sources within the "host" countries (not including the profits that the firms obtained and reinvested in Latin America, which accounted for another 60 percent of their investment funds).[4]

Beyond an overall lack of funds, Latin American dependence also involves a lack of effective organizational strength by local capitalists. The essence of business power is the ability to use funds to control and effectively organize work activity and social, political, and economic institutions in such a way as to enhance both profits and the general accumulation process. The operation of such power requires the firm cohesion of capitalists as a class, the development of their ability to structure economic life in their own interest— which is to say it requires a well-established domination of society by the capitalist class.

Imperialist domination in Latin America and throughout the third world has perverted the development of the local capitalist class. In the colonial era, the authorities explicitly restricted industrial development, reserving the market as far as possible for exports from Europe. Later, when free trade "simply crushed local industry," it also effectively crushed the emergence of a local industrially based capitalist class. Typically, the capitalist classes that have emerged under the long-established domination of foreign capital have been heavily dependent either on the state apparatus, on foreign capital, or on both. Consequently, they have in general not developed the effective national institutions, the social patterns, and the business practices that would give them the power to organize for independent development.

For a capitalist class to lead a national development process, it must be able to use the state. The state in turn must be able to raise revenues for constructing and organizing the nation's physical infrastructure toward internal development, to maintain the stability of the financial system, to support research and development, to establish the orderly operation of labor markets, and, not least, to protect the national market from incursion and domination by foreign business. Yet foreign domination in Latin America, both in the colonial and postcolonial periods, has prevented the state from effectively performing these functions. In some instances, the state could not act because if it did so it would come face to face with foreign interests—as it would if it tried to protect the domestic market. In other instances, the state could not play its role because it did not have sufficient control over revenues: traditional elite groups (particularly landed interests and merchants), whose power was based on economic ties to international trade and investment, were unwilling to finance development projects. Most generally, the capitalist classes found greater advantage in opting for ties—ties of subordination, to be sure—with foreign capital, rather than striking an independent course.

For example, investors in the periphery continually turn to the center as a source of new technology. At any moment, it is more profitable to adopt organizational techniques and equipment developed in the advanced countries than to build on indigenous resources and experience. As a result, in key sectors of the economies of Latin America, national capital is unable to compete with the multinationals and, indeed, welcomes entrance by the foreign firms.

In much of Latin America in the middle of the twentieth

century governments took on a "developmentalist" role, organizing investment and encouraging import-substituting industrialization. In doing so, however, they reinforced their economies' ties to international capital. When, for example, they protected their domestic markets from imports, they also encouraged the entry of foreign firms to produce inside their borders. When import substitution ran its course, they turned to export promotion, strengthening their reliance on foreign markets to propel growth. Without strong national capitalist classes, the countries of Latin America have maintained their position of dependence in the international system. It is a social dependence—or class dependence—as well as a financial dependence.*

The great inequalities in Latin America—the bipolar social structure that is the region's colonial heritage—have also played a major role in shaping development. In the modern era, economic growth has been based on, and has exacerbated, inequality. In Brazil, for example, during the late 1960s and early 1970s, while output per worker in manufacturing rose by 90 percent, real wages dropped by 12 percent. The limited data on income distribution over time suggest that during the post-World War II period, when high growth rates were achieved in Latin America, they were accompanied by increasing income inequality.[5] The pattern is one that assures profits, and even allows Latin American industry to compete with some success in international markets. But it

---

*It is of course possible for a developmentalist state to pursue a different sort of path, as the experience of Japan clearly demonstrates. In the late nineteenth century, and again after World War II, the Japanese state organized development by maintaining strict limits on the activities of foreigners. After World War II, for example, while Latin America and Europe were welcoming U.S.-based multinationals, Japan limited foreign investment and gained access to foreign technology through licensing agreements. South Korea seems to provide an example more in line with the Japanese experience than with that of Latin America. These different paths, however, are not explained by different choices per se, but instead have their roots in different histories and different class development.

is also a pattern that assures mass poverty and thus limits the extent to which domestic savings can provide the funds for further development and domestic spending can provide an adequate market.

Furthermore, in social systems characterized by extreme inequality, the survival of the various elite groups at the top is always in question. The threat of rebellion, if not revolution, by those on the bottom is an ongoing one. Consequently, the elites are required to maintain a formidable bureaucratic and military apparatus to control their own populations. Such an extensive apparatus of control and coercion is, however, a costly drain on national resources, resources that might otherwise be directed toward economic growth.

At the same time that inequality limits the possibilities for economic growth based on internal resources and markets, it makes growth a political imperative. Even with relatively large bureaucratic and military forces, the elites in Latin America must strive to establish economic growth in order to maintain social stability. Economic growth is not only the means for expanding the wealth of those at the top, but it is also the most effective way to prevent middle level groups, who would otherwise suffer from the severe inequality, from entering the opposition. (Indeed, even among the poorest groups, growth holds out a promise of change that limits the gains of oppositional political movements.) The successes of Brazil's military, and especially of Mexico's elite, in preserving their positions of power and privilege owe as much to economic expansion as to repression. Instability in Argentina, where repression has certainly not been lacking, can be traced to a continuing poor economic record.

In a number of ways, then, extreme inequality, part of the region's historical legacy, generates growing dependence. With extreme inequality, the masses of the population are too poverty-stricken to provide either a base for savings or a strong internal market; the elites' own spending on lavish

living, along with the expenditures on extensive bureaucratic-military machines, leaves insufficient funds to
drive investment forward. Consequently, to achieve growth—
made all the more necessary because of the extreme inequality—Brazil, Mexico, and other Latin American nations have
cultivated export markets and generally welcomed foreign
investment.

Bringing the self-perpetuation of inequality and dependence full circle, external dependence buttresses the system
of inequality. Politically, investors from the center (along with
their governments) support the power and privilege of the
elites. As evidence and illustration, one need point only to
the relationship between U.S. interests—government and
business—and the ascendancy of the military regimes in
Brazil and Chile, to say nothing of the situation in Central
America.* Economically, investors from the center introduce
technology that generates minimal employment and direct
their sales toward the market created by the elites' expenditures. Thus the dependency-inequality structure that pre-
dominates in Latin America is a self-reinforcing structure,
and—the key point of emphasis here—it generates a growth
process that relies heavily on imported capital.

Changing Patterns of Dependence

During the period from World War II through the late
1960s, foreign investment coming into Latin America was

---

*U.S. interests are also capable of recognizing that military governments
may not always provide the best means to support the status quo of elite
power and privilege. Like rats leaving the sinking ship, the U.S. government
abandons its client dictators when their fall is imminent and wraps itself in
the banner of democracy—at least until the forces of social reform begin to
make progress.

primarily in the form of direct investment of multinational firms based in the United States, Europe, and Japan. Funds coming in as foreign loans were relatively less important. In that period, however, at least within some of the Latin American nations—Brazil and Mexico are the prime examples— national industry, both state-owned and private, became relatively well established. These new developments did not constitute a break in the relationship between national and international capital, however, because the former remained in its subordinate role and retained its perverted character. National industry did not replace the multinationals, but it did grow up alongside them, often in a supportive or symbiotic relation. In Brazil, for example, the multinationals dominated auto production, but national capital became active in several industries that supply the auto producers and in construction (building roads, among other things). State-owned enterprises dominated several aspects of energy production and distribution and also became important in the steel industry. Further, in some instances multinational, state, and national capital combined in large and complex projects—chemical production in Brazil provides an example.

Nonetheless, in spite of the complementary and often cooperative relation between international and Latin American capital, developments in the 1970s marked a potentially significant alteration in the condition of national capital, at least in the larger and more economically successful Latin American nations. While a break with dependency did not take place, a new form of center-periphery relationship emerged, making some new form of economic development at least conceivable.[6]

The growing role of enterprises owned by Latin American nationals and governments altered the *form* in which capital from abroad was needed. Instead of only foreign direct investment (i.e., from multinationals), in the early 1970s nationally based firms began to pull in increasing amounts of loan capital from large banks in New York, London, Frankfurt, and Tokyo. Thus while Latin America's dependence on foreign investment is nothing new, based as it is on the "pull" produced by the long-established structure of inequality and dependence, the current dependence on financial capital is a form that has its origins in relatively recent developments.*

While the basic "pull" of foreign funds into Latin America has deep historical roots, and while the current form of that pull has roots in the post-World War II era, additional pulls came into being in the 1970s as the international crisis matured. The most widely noted factor was the huge increase in oil prices in 1973. Especially for Brazil, but also for several other nations in the region, maintaining growth meant importing oil, and importing oil meant borrowing hard currency to pay for it. Oil-price increases did not initiate debt problems, but after both 1973 and 1979 (when there was an additional sharp increase) oil-price increases made the problems considerably more severe for several nations.[7]

The "pull" continued to grow in the 1970s, as Latin American countries fueled economic growth with a rapidly increasing level of imports and relied on an increasing volume of loans to finance obligations on previous foreign investment. For the years immediately leading into the debt crisis, the situation is shown in Table 3. The overall balance of payments for Latin America is broken down into the mer-

---

*There have been earlier periods in Latin American history when financial capital played a similarly important role. In the nineteenth century, before the era of the multinational corporation, loans played a relatively large role in the region's foreign dependency. In the late 1920s, leading into the Great Depression, foreign loans to Latin American countries were substantial, setting things up for the defaults of the 1930s. Thus the growing role of national firms in Latin America during recent decades is not the only factor that can lead to a rise in financial connections. Among other things, conditions in the center, which push funds into the periphery, are important, as I stressed earlier.

Table 3
Latin America and the Caribbean:
Balance of Payments on Current Account, 1978–82*
(billions of dollars)

	Overall balance	Trade	Investment income	Other†
1978	− 17.9	− 3.3	− 10.6	− 4.0
1979	− 20.5	− 0.2	− 15.3	− 5.0
1980	− 29.5	1.5	− 20.3	− 10.7
1981	− 42.3	− 2.3	− 30.1	− 9.9
1982	− 39.3	7.1	− 36.3	− 10.5

*Does not include Cuba.

†Includes freight and insurance, travel, private remittances, and items not listed elsewhere.

Source: Inter-American Development Bank, *Economic and Social Progress in Latin America—External Debt: Crisis and Adjustment* (Washington D.C., 1985), Tables 41–48.

chandise trade balance, the net flow of investment income, and an "other" category. For the region as a whole, there was no serious trade imbalance in these years, but between 1978 and 1981 the balance of payments deficit grew by 136 percent. This growth in the deficit was largely accounted for by the growth in the net outflow of investment income (profits and interest).*

Even as economic growth waned in the center, Latin American governments met the growth imperative through the

---

*There are, of course, differences among the countries of the region. It is worth noting, however, that the differences do not neatly separate the oil-exporting countries from the rest of the group. The oil-price increase of 1979 created a fairly favorable situation in Venezuela's balance of payments, but Mexico's balance of payments deficit continued to grow as rapidly as did that of the whole region over the 1978–81 period.

1970s by taking on larger and larger volumes of debt. The debt, however, created an obligation, and as export markets weakened in the early 1980s, growth could be maintained in Latin America only by an increasingly rapid escalation of borrowing. By the beginning of the decade it was widely recognized that if expansion in the center was not re-established, the growth attained in Latin America through borrowing would only postpone the day of reckoning. In addition, continuing inflation and instability in the center imposed extremely high interest rates on the debtor nations, making the entire financial system more precarious.

Then, as the slow growth of the late 1970s turned into the severe recession of the early 1980s, the day of reckoning came. The current crisis in Latin America—with default scares, debt renegotiations, and "conditionality" agreements, declining output and austerity programs, political turmoil and riots—appeared in full form.

Power in the Crisis

The current crisis marks a considerable setback for national development in Latin America. The growing role of state and national capital in Brazil, Mexico, and elsewhere did not involve a break from the region's history of dependence. Nonetheless, changes since the 1960s were a threat to the old system of power that dominated the international economy after World War II. The growing strength of national capital in the Latin American nations was closely connected to the decline of U.S. hegemony.

In the some twenty years after World War II, there was virtually no effective challenge to the operation of U.S. business and the U.S. government, both within the international capitalist economy generally and within Latin America particularly. In Latin America there was considerable nationalist rhetoric and popular feeling for limiting the role of U.S. corporations. Even where nationalism appeared powerful, however, the policies of that era accommodated to the interests of the multinational corporations. The U.S.-based firms, with their control of capital and technology and with the political leverage exercised by the U.S. government, met only limited resistance. Nationalists, who were driven by the growth imperative and who accepted the general framework of capitalism, had little choice but to turn to U.S. firms. In Brazil, for example, nationalist rhetoric was but a limited barrier to the establishment of "Instruction 113" which, through preferential exchange-rate treatment, gave a decided advantage to foreign investors over national capital.[8] Elsewhere, as in Bolivia, a reliance on foreign finance created a "debt-trap" (portending the wider situation in the 1980s); as a nationalist government became dependent on loans from the IMF, it was forced to comply with the interests of the multinationals.[9] It certainly appeared that national capitalist development was not a real option; national capital, it seemed, could and would always do better for itself by welcoming foreign capital and accepting a subordinate role—and through the 1950s and on into the 1960s, foreign capital almost always meant U.S. capital.

In retrospect, however, it is clear that even in the decades of extreme U.S. power in Latin America, changes were taking place. In the late 1950s and 1960s, governments in the region took steps to force U.S. firms to transform long-standing sales, service, and assembly operations into full-fledged manufacturing facilities. They also nationalized public utility and natural resource-based investments, and required local participation in ownership.[10] In themselves, such events were not a threat to the power of U.S. capital in Latin America. Yet they were the beginning of a process that, under altered international circumstances, would take on considerable force. Moreover, as economic growth did take place in Latin America, largely through import substitution and under the aegis of penetration by U.S. capital, both national capitalist classes and the economic roles of the state expanded considerably.

In the late 1960s and early 1970s, international circumstances began to change. With the demise of the Bretton Woods international monetary arrangements in 1971, one could speak of the end of U.S. hegemony. In terms of economic change in Latin America, the end of U.S. hegemony meant that national forces were less constrained in pursuing their favored development policies, and that the direct influence of the U.S. government in affecting these policies was considerably weakened. More important, however, U.S.-based firms now faced considerable competition from Japanese- and European-based rivals, allowing greater leverage to Latin American forces in their dealings with the multinationals. (Also, a greater number of U.S. firms had developed international operations, contributing to the competition among the multinationals.)

One manifestation of the new situation was the increasing frequency with which joint ownership arrangements were imposed on the multinationals. Brazil's experience with joint ventures stands out, but available data suggest similar tendencies in Colombia and Mexico, as well as elsewhere in the third world.[11] In addition, even with "high tech" industries, the new situation gave Latin American governments greater leverage, allowing them to insist, for example, on local content and export requirements as conditions for computer firms to set up production facilities and gain access to the growing local market; Mexico's success with various computer firms is an illustration of this.[12] An increase in the nationalizations of U.S. firms in the third world was still another sign of the new circumstances, with the experience of the oil industry—in Venezuela, for example—as the over-shadowing case.[13]

The point here is not that these sorts of change resulted in great losses for the multinationals. As the case of oil illustrates, they have been able to adjust to the new situation fairly well, at least in the short run. Their profits and, through their control of markets and technology, much of their power have been maintained. Yet the implications of these changes cannot be discounted. Within Latin America, the growing power and organizational capacity of national capital, always in concert with the state apparatus, has been considerable.

These developments have a parallel in a previous period of Latin America's history. During the early nineteenth century conflict and disarray in Europe (the center) facilitated great change in Latin America (the periphery). Latin America was not able to break out of its subordinate position in the international economy, but its position changed as colonialism in the region was virtually eliminated. A well-ordered subordination was only reestablished as the century proceeded and British hegemony became firmly entrenched. In the current era, the decline of U.S. hegemony and the associated disorder and rivalry in the center have once again facilitated change in the Latin American periphery. It would be wrong to expect this change to move unabated in the direction of greater power and autonomy for Latin America; but it would also be a mistake to ignore the reality of the change.

It is in this context that the debt crisis has descended upon Latin America. With the advance of national forces in the region so dependent on the flow of financial capital from the center, the crisis in that flow of funds upsets that advance. In order to extricate themselves from the debt crisis, Latin American governments are being forced to accept conditions that run contrary to their national development programs. There should be no mistake about the fact that, as far as human suffering is concerned, it is the poorest groups in Latin America that bear the brunt of the austerity programs that are being imposed by the IMF and the private banks. Yet the "conditionality" that accompanies new loans from the center includes much more than austerity. Latin American governments are being pressured to ease regulations on the inflow of foreign investment (e.g., to ease joint venture and export requirements), to reduce currency controls that might be used to insulate and protect national development, and to abandon stimulatory fiscal policies. Moreover, they are being pushed to rededicate their economies toward export promotion as the route to growth. The programs being pushed on the periphery by the central powers in their effort to resolve the debt crisis thus amount to a counteroffensive against national development.[14]

One of the goals of this counteroffensive, a goal embraced by many conservative forces in Latin America as well as by the U.S. government and the IMF, is a shrinkage in the economic role played by the government. Along with the greater openings for foreign investment and trade, conditionality agreements stress "privatization"—the selling-off of government enterprises—and cutbacks in public service expenditures. However, the debt crisis is also bringing an intensification of class struggle and extreme disruptions of economic activity, both of which push the governments of the region in the direction of more, not less, involvement in their economies.

The growing intensity of class struggle (to which I will return in Chapter 5) is likely to bring larger and more direct economic roles for governments, as the elites turn to an enhanced bureaucratic-military apparatus to preserve their dominance. Such action, as has traditionally been the case, will involve both repression and reform. Repression is as much an economic as a political phenomenon, partly because it is brought to bear against workers and peasants demanding economic change and partly because it uses resources, creates jobs, and involves state economic planning. Reforms will involve governments in direct intervention in the economy to limit the havoc and disruption that the market, under pressure from the outflow of resources to pay the debt, necessarily creates.

Class struggle aside, however, the debt crisis is having its most severe impact on the weakest segments of the private economy, namely on those enterprises that are in the hands of national capital. In a few instances foreign capital may enter to pick up the pieces when national capital fails, but by and large multinational firms are not attracted to those segments of the economy where national firms are concentrated—the more competitive, labor-intensive, small-scale operations. Consequently, to avoid severe disruption, governments are likely to provide more support for weak national operations.

It seems likely that the ideological proclivities of IMF advisors, the U.S. government, and free market conservatives in Latin America may not be a match for the realities of the situation. Free markets may have their role in history, but establishing stability is not one of them. Whatever else these groups want, they want stability. Moreover, in Brazil, Mexico, and elsewhere, the state's role in the economy has become entrenched over the decades. To move toward a free market solution, governments in Latin America would need to dismantle a large bureaucratic apparatus, a process that might be politically unfeasible and economically disastrous.

The debt crisis in Latin America is far from over, and there is no ready way to predict how the various struggles—between national forces and imperial power, between different capitalist forces within the region, and between classes—will be resolved. It is clear, however, that the debt crisis has set in motion changes with historic dimensions.

4

Financial Shift: The Growth of U.S. Foreign Debt and Trade Problems

There could hardly be a more popular precept of economics than that the powerful are creditors and the weak are debtors. The classic image of the debtor is the small farmer or homeowner beholden to a rich banker. The third world debt crisis fits the pattern well, with the world's poor nations teetering under the burden of obligations to creditors far away in the centers of wealth and power. Of course, as with many popular precepts reality is a bit more complicated. Many large and powerful firms have built corporate empires on the basis of debt; the very rich take out mortgages on their mansions; and in the nineteenth century, the United States became an industrial power by using foreign debt. Nonetheless, between individuals as between countries, there is a great deal of truth in the idea that strength comes with being a creditor and weakness is the lot of the debtor.

So it is no small matter that during the 1980s the United States switched from being the world's largest creditor to its largest debtor. The United States became an international creditor during World War I, and its creditor role grew substantially during the interwar years. In the aftermath of World War II—during this era of U.S. hegemony—the overwhelming role of U.S. firms as investors and the leading financial role of the government were almost synonymous with U.S. power. Thus when change came in the 1980s, it was far more than a matter of accounting.

Figure 4.1 traces the net international investment position of the United States between 1960 and 1988. This is the value of U.S.-owned assets abroad less the value of foreign-owned assets in the United States. These data (like most sets of aggregate statistics) have their shortcomings, and one should not place great weight on the particular numbers. Nevertheless, even if the absolute values of the numbers are not very accurate, the general picture of great change in the 1980s is surely real.*

Through the 1960s, as the world economy expanded with U.S. firms in the forefront, the investment position of the United States moved upward substantially. But in the early 1970s, the instability associated with the demise of U.S. hegemony begins to appear in the data. In 1971 and 1972,

---

*The figures include assets held as direct (equity) investments, assets held as long- and short-term financial investments, and government assets. U.S. government holdings of monetary gold stocks are counted as a foreign assets because, like the currency of another country or a foreign bond, the gold can be used directly as a claim on real foreign assets. The problems with the data are substantial. To begin with, U.S. gold holdings are greatly under-valued, counted as \$11.1 billion in 1987, for example, when their market value would be closer to \$100 billion. Also, both U.S. direct investments abroad and foreign direct investment in the United States are listed at "book value"—that is, the value at which those assets were purchased less de-preciation. The use of book values increasingly understates market values (or replacement values) of assets as assets age. Since U.S. direct investments abroad are on average older than foreign-held assets in the United States, the effect of using book values is to overstate the degree to which the United States is a net debtor. Correct valuation of both gold and direct invest-ments—i.e., valuation at replacement values—would make the United States less of a net debtor (and more of a net creditor in the earlier years). In the other direction, "errors and omissions" in the international accounts include substantial additional foreign investments in the United States, and their inclusion would make the United States more of net debtor. All in all, the official figures make the United States appear more of a debtor than it actually is.

Figure 4.1

*Net International Investment Position of the U.S., 1960–88
(U.S. assets abroad less foreign assets
in the United States in billions of dollars)*

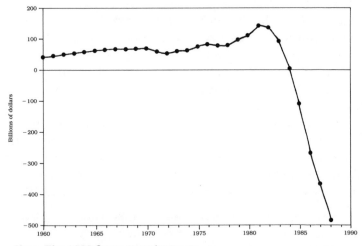

Note: The 1988 figure is preliminary.

Source: *Federal Reserve Bulletin*, May 1989; *The Economic Report of the President, 1989; Survey of Current Business*, August 1980 and early years; *Historical Statistics of the United States: Colonial Times to 1970* (Washington, D.C.: U.S. Department of Commerce, Bureau of the Census, 1975).

the U.S. investment position took a sharp (though small by later standards) downward turn in connection with the demise of the Bretton Woods system.* After 1974, however, the earlier upward trend reappeared as U.S. international banking expansion began to pick up steam.

---

*The actual mechanism by which the net international investment position of the United States fell in the early 1970s involved extensive action by both private interests and governments. As private investors saw the coming decline in the value of the dollar, they moved their assets to other currencies. This in itself would have raised the net investment position of the United States. However, as I explained in Chapter 2, in an effort to keep the value of

Then, in the late 1970s and early 1980s, more dramatic changes took place as U.S. banks greatly increased their international investments—primarily loans to the third world. Between 1978 and 1981 the net international invest-ment position of the United States rose by 85 percent, to its peak of $141 billion. As the debt crisis emerged and the banks stopped increasing their foreign loans, however, the situation did not return to pre-1978 conditions. Something new happened. Foreign interests began to purchase U.S. assets at an unprecedented rate, and the net international investment position of the United States plummeted. By the end of 1988, the United States was a net international debtor to the tune of nearly $500 billion (although, as noted in the first footnote in this chapter, the precise magnitude of the change is subject to question).

Although the international investment role of the United States changed dramatically in the 1980s, the forces leading to the change had been building for some time. Like the third world debt that it followed, U.S. international debt arose in large part as a response to the relative stagnation and instability of the international economy. What's more, as the third world debt was in part (its "push" part) a con-sequence of the U.S. government's macroeconomic policies, so the build-up of U.S. debt followed from those same poli-cies. In both cases, these policies played a major role in shaping the impact of stagnation and instability. The story of the U.S. international debt build-up in the 1980s is therefore something of a sequel to the third world debt build-up of the 1970s.

Financial affairs sometimes seem far removed from peo-

---

the dollar from falling and the values of their own currencies from rising, foreign governments and central banks purchased a huge amount of dollars with their own currencies. Thus through 1970, 1971, and 1972, foreign official agencies greatly increased their holdings of dollar assets, leading to a net fall in the international investment position of the United States.

ple's daily lives and immediate problems. Of course, in Latin America and elsewhere in the third world, the impact of finance is, unfortunately, all too apparent. In the United States people have some awareness of general financial problems as high interest rates have become a costly and often disruptive fact of life, especially since the late 1970s. The social impact of U.S. financial problems, however, has a much more dramatic, although indirect, effect. The huge U.S. trade deficit, the loss of employment in many industries, and the depressing impact of international competition on wages are closely connected to the rising debt. The U.S. debt story is coupled with the U.S. trade dislocation story, and in this chapter I will say something about the latter as well as the former.

U.S. Macroeconomic Policy in the 1980s

A large part of the economic history of the last twenty years could be written as the story of U.S. government efforts to find ways to restore both order and U.S. power in the international economy. Through the 1970s, the focus of these efforts was on new forms of international cooperation, as the United States tried to get the Japanese and Europeans to play the role of partner—though certainly junior partners—in regulating world capitalism. This was the strategy of "Trilateralism," which found its symbolic expression in annual meetings, beginning in 1975, among the heads of state of the seven leading capitalist powers (the United States, Japan, Britain, West Germany, France, Italy, and Canada). Although these meetings served primarily as public relations affairs, their formal purpose was to work out common, coordinated policies for dealing with economic instability.

Early efforts to achieve cooperation met with little success, as the various governments pursued their own particular policies during the first oil-price increase and in the serious recession of 1974–75. The need for cooperation did not subside after the mid-decade downturn, and from the point of view of the United States in the late 1970s there was an increasing need to have other governments play a larger role in stabilizing the international economy. Facing the nasty combination of high unemployment and high inflation, the U.S. government had very limited macroeconomic policy options. It could do little about inflation without making unemployment worse and vice-versa. So the Carter administration turned to the West German and Japanese governments, attempting to have them expand their spending programs and thereby provide more stimulus to the world economy. In the idiom of the period, West Germany and Japan were to be the "locomotives" of the international economy. The West Germans and the Japanese had their own agendas, however, and these did not include providing substantial fiscal stimulation for the international system. In reality, then, Trilateralism did not go much beyond professions of good intentions, and the U.S. and world economies limped along toward the 1980s.

Trilateralism was thoroughly attacked by right-wing forces in the United States as a betrayal of U.S. interests, a retreat from the country's position of power in world affairs. Indeed, at the 1976 Republican National Convention, Henry Kissinger was assailed for having made a statement acknowledging the decline of U.S. international power. With the ascendancy of Ronald Reagan to the presidency in 1981, the emphasis in foreign policy—political and economic—shifted to an effort to restore U.S. hegemony.

The move away from Trilateralism, however, was not simply the result of the Reagan presidential victory. Causation was at least partially in the other direction, as the failure of a cooperative, or power sharing, approach to international affairs contributed to Reagan's electoral success. Moreover, one of the key steps back toward U.S. unilateralism had been taken in late 1979 when the Federal Reserve, under the direction of Paul Volcker, had initiated a highly restrictive monetary policy. This policy was designed to restore the international value of the dollar and bring stability to international financial markets. Also, "tight money" would serve to curb domestic inflation, raise unemployment, and shift economic power away from workers and toward employers. The Volcker initiative was the first element of what came to be identified as the Reagan macroeconomic policies. Yet Volcker had been appointed by Carter, and, despite opposition within the administration, his position defined the government's policy.*

It was, however, only with the advent of the Reagan era that the policy of monetary restriction became part of a comprehensive political and economic program to create a new era of unilateral U.S. power. The program, which had domestic as well as international objectives, meant that the U.S. government would pursue macroeconomic policies that were highly detrimental to the stability of the international economy; other governments would be forced to adjust. In addition, the attempt to restore U.S. power would involve a huge increase in military expenditure. U.S. dominance after World War II had been based on military as well as economic supremacy, and the Reagan policies sought to restore su-

*Volcker's 1979 actions were not in themselves unilateral U.S. actions. Indeed, the U.S. government was being pushed by other governments to take action to stabilize the dollar. Those actions, however, began a policy by which the U.S. would run large international trade and financial imbalances during the 1980s and other nations would be forced to adjust under the pressure of those imbalances. On the events surrounding the implementation of Volcker's policy, see William Greider, *Secrets of the Temple: How the Federal Reserve Runs the Country* (New York: Simon and Schuster, 1987), pp. 116–23.

premacy through a military build-up and through the aggressive pursuit, often in the face of objections from allies, of a foreign policy that would reestablish U.S. authority in the third world and place continual pressure on the Soviet Union.

In its early years, the Reagan administration pursued its program by the unusual combination of large federal budget deficits and the tight money policies of the Federal Reserve. This peculiar policy mix followed partly from the administration's international goals and partly from its domestic goals; the latter had at their core an upward redistribution of income. Budget deficits were dictated by the administration's commitment to the otherwise contradictory goals of a rapid escalation of military spending and a reduction of taxes. Given the deficits, tight money was the only policy by which an inflation-reducing recession could then be induced. While the deficits created a strong demand for credit, monetary policy restricted its supply. The result was to be expected: very high real interest rates. Those high interest rates had their intended impact when they precipitated the severe recession of 1982.

More important for the discussion here, the high interest rates drew foreign funds into the United States, as foreign investors demanded dollars in order to purchase U.S. securities and take advantage of the high returns. The important factor, of course, was not simply that interest rates were high, but that interest rates in the United States were high relative to interest rates in the other advanced capitalist countries. Figure 4.2 shows the movement of real long-term interest rates in the United States and abroad from the mid-1970s through the mid-1980s. (In the figure, the foreign interest rate is a weighted average of the interest rates in other major industrial countries.) In the late 1970s, U.S. real interest rates were running below foreign interest rates, and were even negative for some years (i.e., the rate of inflation

Figure 4.2
*Real Long-Term Interest Rates in the United States
and Abroad, 1976–87**

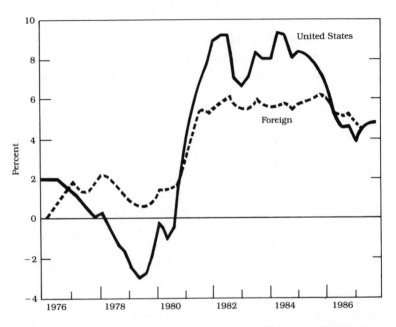

*This figure is reproduced from U.S. Congress, Senate and House Committees on the Budget, *The Economic and Budget Outlook: Fiscal Years 1989–93*, Part I, Congressional Budget Office, February 1988. In computing the real interest rate, expected inflation is proxied by a two-year centered moving average of actual and projected Consumer Price Index inflation figures. The foreign interest rate is a gross domestic product-weighted average of the rates of other major industrial countries.

was higher than the interest rate). But with the tight money policies initiated in 1979, U.S. rates leaped upward, rising above foreign rates by 1981 and staying above them until 1986. The macroeconomic policies of the early 1980s, then, drew foreign funds into the United States and began the transformation of the United States from international creditor to international debtor.*

In a second phase of the implementation of its policy, which coincided roughly with its second term, the Reagan administration maintained the stimulus of large deficits but eased monetary policy. The large deficits had helped pull the economy out of the 1982 recession, and with the easing of monetary policy growth continued: moderate growth by the standards of modern history but rapid growth by comparison with most of the rest of the world (see Table 4, page 95). Moreover, the policies of the two phases were at least a partial success in one crucial area: profit rates in the United States rose substantially following the 1982 recession. Moderate growth with relatively high unemployment appears to have been good for U.S. firms.

The high interest rates that had been established in the first phase of the Reagan policy were maintained in the second phase (though by 1986 they had fallen a bit and were roughly equivalent to foreign rates—see Figure 4.2). Add to this the continuation of a strong fiscal stimulus, high profit rates, the favorable political context (from the point of view of investors), and the continuing importance of the dollar in international affairs, and the results are easy to understand. The United States in the 1980s was a haven for capital. The strong movement of funds into the United States, the purchase of U.S. assets by foreign interests, and the move away from creditor toward debtor status thus continued.

The macroeconomic policies of the Reagan administration

---

*While relatively high interest rates were drawing investments to the United States from Europe and Japan, funds were also coming in from Latin America. As that region's debt crisis brought general economic devastation, wealthy individuals moved billions of dollars to the haven of U.S. banks. Thus we have a direct, and ironic, connection between the Latin American debt crisis and one part of the U.S. debt expansion.

Figure 4.3
U.S. Trade Balance, 1946–88

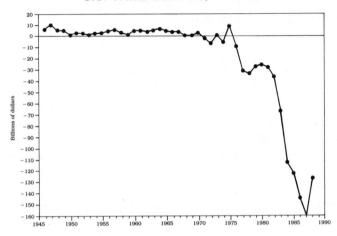

Figure 4.4
U.S. Trade Balance as a Percentage
of Gross National Product, 1946–88

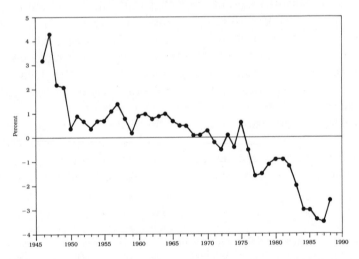

Source: *Economic Report of the President, 1989* and *Federal Reserve Bulletin,* May 1989.

during the 1980s, particularly the large fiscal deficits that were a central and constant feature of those policies, were the proximate cause of the build-up of the U.S. foreign debt. The deficits can in turn be seen as the government's unilateral response to international economic instability and stagnation. Without a basis for the expansion of productive investment and self-sustaining growth, the government sought to induce economic growth by piling up deficits and debt. In doing so, it exacerbated the instability of its own international economic relations—an instability that feeds into all aspects of economic life.

The Impact on Trade

The large capital movements that make up international debt and the associated shifts in exchange rates, to which I will turn shortly, provide one measure of international instability. Another measure is provided by the huge and unprecedented shift in the U.S. balance of international trade, and it is through trade that the financial shift has had its most immediate and harshest impact on people's lives.

The Rising Trade Problem in the 1970s. In 1971, for the first time in the twentieth century, the United States imported more merchandise than it exported. Up until then the country's trade surplus—like its creditor status—had been an important symbol of power in the world economy. The shift to deficit status was an equally important symbol of change, and since 1971 the United States has registered trade deficits in all but two years. Figure 4.3 shows the aggregate trade balance on U.S. merchandise trade for the years 1946 through 1988, and Figure 4.4 provides a comparison of the trade balance to GNP.*

The aggregate data in Figures 4.3 and 4.4 hide as much as they reveal, however, for the trade deficit was not evenly spread over all categories of goods. Up into the 1980s, the deficit was accounted for largely by oil and by one category of manufactured goods, automobiles. Without oil and the auto trade, there is no deficit prior to the severe dislocation of the mid-1980s and, of special importance, there is no downward trend in the balance prior to 1981.[1]†

Within manufacturing sectors, there was a highly varied

---

*The 1975 trade surplus is worth comment because it is such a good reminder that a trade surplus does not necessarily imply anything positive about the general state of an economy. The severe U.S. recession of that year meant that the demand for imports was very weak; the value of imports actually fell by some 5 percent between 1974 and 1975 (an especially large decline because import prices rose by 7 percent over the two years). At the same time, although the recession of the mid-1970s was an international recession, U.S. trading partners were not as severely affected and thus the demand for U.S. exports was maintained. Consequently, the trade surplus that appeared in 1975 was the reflection of a relatively weak economy, not a sign of economic strength.

†Disaggregation of the trade balance is useful for descriptive purposes, but can be misleading since all components of trade are interdependent. For example, consider the large import of oil in the 1970s as a given. This means that the United States was supplying a large amount of dollars to foreign sources to pay for oil imports. The large supply of dollars (i.e., the large import of oil) meant that the dollar had a lower value in terms of other currencies than it otherwise would have had. Thus, the cost of foreign goods—e.g., German machine tools—in terms of dollars was higher than it otherwise would have been and imports were consequently less than they otherwise would have been. Similarly, the cost to foreigners of U.S. chemicals, for example, was less than it would otherwise have been, and exports of chemicals were greater than they would otherwise have been. Accordingly, it makes no sense to say something like, "Without the large imports of oil, the U.S. would have run trade surpluses in the 1970s," because without the large imports of oil everything else would have been different. Nonetheless, the disaggregation does allow us to get a better picture of what was going on.

set of experiences, but there is a pattern to the variation: in the 1970s the United States ran substantial surpluses in capital goods, chemicals, and military goods, while experiencing deficits in manufactured consumer goods. This was a change from the earlier postwar period, when the United States had run trade surpluses in all categories of manufactured goods, but it was not a change from widespread surpluses to widespread deficits.[2]

What distinguishes consumer goods from other types of manufactures is the size of the markets and the nature of the production processes. In general, the market for any given consumer good, such as TV sets or blue jeans, is larger than for other types of manufactured goods, such as airplanes or machine tools. The large market for a standardized product facilitates the development of mass production techniques that make heavy use of relatively unskilled, low-wage labor. Thus what we saw in the changing pattern of U.S. trade in the 1970s was a move toward a reliance on foreign sources for that production which involved a relatively high quantity of low-wage labor.

In addition to these shifting trade patterns, there was also a substantial increase in the overall importance of international trade for the U.S. economy. Between 1970 and 1980, imports jumped from 3.9 percent of GNP to 9.1 percent and exports from 4.2 percent to 8.2 percent. This increase in the "openness" of the economy was set in motion by the success of U.S. power during the postwar years in laying the foundation for a more highly integrated international economy. Then, in the late 1960s and 1970s, as postwar recovery was completed abroad, modern facilities came "on-line" in many countries. Foreign firms began to penetrate U.S. markets more effectively, and U.S. firms made more extensive use of their foreign subsidiaries to supply the home market. These changes took place within a context of declining growth rates throughout the world economy and a general intensification of international competition, which led to a greater inter-penetration of U.S. and foreign markets.

The combination of these changes in the 1970s—the increasing openness of the economy and the shift toward importing goods produced with low-wage labor—placed certain categories of workers in the United States under increasing pressure from international competition. In general, these workers were people engaged in mass production activity; their jobs had been successfully "deskilled" and technology had been standardized. Poorly paid U.S. workers engaged in such activity—women working in assembly-type operations, for example—had little that would recommend them to an employer over even more poorly paid workers abroad. In addition, workers with a higher level of skill were not safe if they were engaged in a mass production activity whose technology was easily transferable. Workers who had been especially successful in obtaining wage increases were particularly vulnerable. In auto and steel, where strong unions and the monopolistic positions enjoyed for many years by the principal companies had combined to provide relatively high wages, the employment and wages of workers came under severe attack.*

---

*Mainstream economists have presented the U.S. reliance on foreign sources for "low-wage goods" as a "natural" consequence of different availabilities of cheap labor in different parts of the world. However, whether or not a particular good is a "low-wage good"—i.e., what technology is used in its production—is by no means "natural." As Harry Braverman in *Labor and Monopoly Capital* (New York, Monthly Review Press, 1974) and others have pointed out, the choice of technology is part of class struggle. There is also nothing "natural" about the structure of the labor supply in various countries. Whether or not low-wage labor is readily available in a particular country for the production of goods for the U.S. market is a consequence of substantial political and social conflict. In noting the way in which the results of these struggles, as they have previously evolved, appear in the pattern of international trade, we should not fall into the trap of seeing that pattern as "natural" or beyond the realm of new struggles.

What Happened to Trade in the 1980s? While these emerging problems were well recognized by the end of the 1970s, they became much more pronounced in the 1980s as the trade situation changed in a most dramatic fashion. The overall trade deficit ballooned from $25 billion in 1980 to $160 billion in 1987 (see Figures 4.3 and 4.4). When trade in oil and autos is excluded, there was a shift from a $62 billion *surplus* in 1980 to a $62 billion *deficit* in 1985. After 1981, exports stopped growing while imports continued to expand rapidly. The resulting trade deficit was huge (about 70 percent of the value of exports by 1986), historically unprecedented, and widespread. Most categories of manufactured goods showed deficits, capital goods as well as consumer goods.[3]

The extreme trade shifts of the 1980s have at the very least caused considerable short-term hardship for millions of people in the United States. Moreover, when unemployment is both highly visible and directly affected by import competition, it has a far-reaching demonstration effect. People know when a plant has been closed and a community devastated, even if the associated overall rise in the national unemployment rate is negligible. Workers in manufacturing industries can see the impact of increased competition from imports, and their behavior at the bargaining table is affected.

The trade experience of the 1980s is often explained as a continuation of the experience of the 1970s, only more so. According to this interpretation, pressures on certain segments of the economy—auto, steel, manufactured consumer goods—that began to appear in the 1970s simply spread in the 1980s. The trade problems of both decades are then blamed on the weak competitive position of the United States, Japan's allegedly unfair trading practices, a surge of low-wage production in South Korea and Taiwan (part of a new international division of labor), and so forth. However, such phenomena, insofar as they are real, are long-term processes; they do not explain the sudden trade shifts of the 1980s.

In fact, the reasons for the huge trade deficits of the 1980s are readily apparent if we shift our attention back to the huge buildup of U.S. foreign debt. The conditions that generated the debt—high interest rates, strong profits, and relatively strong growth—were also the underlying causes of the trade deficit. The debt and the deficit are thus two sides of the same coin. Foreign interests obtain dollars from sales to the United States (U.S. imports), and these dollars can be used to purchase either U.S. goods and services from the United States (U.S. exports) or U.S. assets. When U.S. assets, rather than U.S. exports, are sold, the U.S. trade deficit and the U.S. international debt expand simultaneously.

One of the important proximate causes that led foreign interests to purchase U.S. assets and produced the trade deficit was the relatively slow growth of demand in the economies of U.S. trading partners. While 30 percent of U.S. exports went to Western Europe in 1980, the annual average growth rate for the European Economic Community (EEC) in the 1981–85 period was only 1.5 percent. In 1980, 37 percent of U.S. exports went to the "developing countries," but as the debt crisis and the turmoil in oil prices disrupted economies of these countries, their average growth rate in the 1981–85 period was reduced to only 1.6 percent.

The important point for explaining the growing U.S. trade deficit of the early 1980s, however, is not just that economic growth slowed in most parts of the world, but that growth slowed more elsewhere than in the United States. Table 4 provides data comparing GNP growth rates for the United States and various groups of other countries since 1965. If we focus our attention on 1981 to 1985, the years of the ballooning U.S. trade deficit, and compare the experiences of different countries, it is evident that there has been relatively *less* slowdown in the U.S. growth rate. For example, in the

Table 4
GNP Growth in Selected Areas Divided by
GNP Growth in the United States × 100

	1966/70	*1971/75*	*1976/80*	*1981/85*	*1984/88*
Canada	153	236	108	108	110
Japan	367	195	147	160	110
European Economic Community	153	132	88	60	63
Developing countries	193	259	147	64	60*

*For 1984–87.

Source: *Economic Report of the President, 1988,* p. 374; and *Economic Report of the President, 1989,* p. 434.

1966–70 period, the EEC's GNP growth rate was 53 percent greater than that of the United States; in 1971–75 it was still 32 percent greater; but in 1976–80 it was 12 percent less; and in 1981–85 it was only 60 percent of that of the United States. A similar, though not so steady, pattern is evident for each country (or country grouping) shown in Table 4. These differences in growth rates did not just "happen," but were the result of the highly expansionary macroeconomic policies of the Reagan years.

One consequence of this differential growth experience was, as I have noted above, the expansion of the U.S. foreign debt as foreign investors put funds in this country. The concomitant consequence for trade was that U.S. demand for foreign goods tended to grow substantially more rapidly than foreign demand for U.S. goods—which is to say that the differential growth rates created a tendency for the U.S. trade deficit to increase in the early 1980s. Had the dollar declined relative to other currencies, the tendency for the U.S. trade deficit to rise (due to the relative increase in the U.S. growth

Figure 4.5
The Real Exchange Rate and the Difference Between
Long-Term Interest Rates in the United States and Abroad,
1976–87*

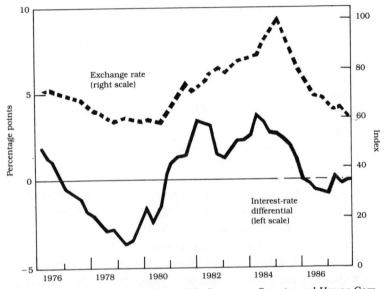

*This figure is reproduced from *U.S. Congress, Senate and House Committees on the Budget, The Economic and Budget Outlook: Fiscal Years 1989–93*, Part I, Congressional Budget Office, February 1988. The real interest rate differential is taken from Figure 4.2. The real exchange rate is a trade-weighted average of dollar exchange rates adjusted for consumer price inflation.

rate) would have been offset by a tendency for the trade deficit to fall (due to a relative decline in the price of U.S. goods).

In fact, the U.S. dollar appreciated substantially during the early 1980s. Overall, when the value of the dollar peaked in the first quarter of 1985, it was 70 percent higher than it had been in the 1978–80 period. Throughout 1984 and 1985, as compared to that earlier period, U.S. exports were 50 percent more expensive for foreign buyers and foreign goods were one-third cheaper for U.S. buyers. Under these circumstances, the growth of the trade deficit is not hard to understand.[4]*

Where did the appreciation in the value of the dollar come from? It was directly linked to the difference between U.S. and foreign interest rates (Figure 4.2). As the interest rate differential attracted funds to the United States, this demand for dollars drove up the value of the dollar. The relationship is clear in Figure 4.5, which shows both the interest rate differential (taken from Figure 4.2) and an index of the real exchange rate: as the interest rate differential shifted in favor of U.S. assets and as funds then flowed to this country, the value of the dollar went up in terms of other currencies.

U.S. Debt and U.S. Power

U.S. debt and U.S. power in the international economy are intertwined, but the connection is certainly not a simple one. The debt expansion did occur in large part as a consequence of the decline in U.S. international power. With the

---

*We would not, however, expect that a decline in the value of the dollar—as has taken place since 1985—would quickly reverse the situation and restore the balance or lead to a surplus. Indeed, the decline in the value of a country's currency often leads to an immediate rise in the deficit because agreements contracted at the old prices are still in effect while imports are now more costly in the home currency. This process is referred to as the "J" curve phenomenon, and the U.S. experience since 1985 seems to fit this pattern. Only in 1988 did a reduction of the trade deficit become evident. In addition to these technical phenomena, which lead to a slow response to exchange rate changes, the fact that so much international trade is intra-firm trade—i.e., from one branch of a multinational firm to another—tends to reduce the speed of response to price changes.

erosion of U.S. hegemony and the emergence of relative stagnation, the government followed macroeconomic and political policies—e.g., the military build-up of the 1980s—in its
attempt to restore both economic stability and U.S. power.
Ironically, the result of these policies has been new instability: the sharp financial shifts and the trade imbalances
that I have been discussing.

At the same time, however, the impact of the government's
economic policies would have been very different if the
United States did not still occupy a position of considerable
power in the world economy. The great size of the U.S. economy and the continuing central role of the dollar in international commerce have allowed policy options that would not
have been available to a lesser power. Extreme fiscal stimulation by the Reagan administration in the 1980s drew funds
to this country. Elsewhere—as in fact was the case in France
during the early years of the Mitterrand government—such
stimulation would have been more likely to have resulted in
capital flight. Thus while the expansion of the U.S. foreign
debt was generated by the decline of U.S. power, it was also
made possible by the continued existence of that same
power.

Still, the direction of the power change seems relatively
clear, and the debt and the trade deficit have further weakened the U.S. position in international affairs. To begin with,
the government's macroeconomic policy options are directly
constrained by the debt-deficit combination and by the high
degree of openness of the U.S. economy. Policy adjustments
in either direction could lead to difficulties. An effort to raise
interest rates and lower GNP growth could, by raising the
fear of recession, trigger substantial movements of capital
out of the country. Alternatively, any move toward lower interest rates, cutting the return on U.S. assets, could also
result in outward capital movement. Were investors to flee
the dollar, a major financial crisis might ensue. None of these
changes are easy to predict, as they are bound up with

inflation, complex expectations, and the general instability of financial markets. But that is the point: the debt-deficit imbalances have both raised the stakes involved in policy adjustment and made the consequences of adjustment all the more difficult to foresee.

On a different plane, the debt and trade imbalances have weakened the international position of many U.S. firms in relation to their European and Japanese rivals. The trade-related devastation of many segments of U.S. industry during the 1980s may have had its most poignant impact upon workers, but many corporations have also been harmed. Bankruptcy rates were high in the 1980s, and in some sectors—steel was a visible example—large factories were shut down at considerable cost. Many companies have, of course, protected themselves by establishing production facilities abroad. Others have adjusted through complex restructuring, involving extensive mechanization and subcontracting. Yet these adjustments have been accompanied by the ceding of a larger and larger share of the U.S. market to foreign rivals; consumer electronics is a prominent example. In recent years, the share of the U.S. market supplied by imports has stopped rising, but at the same time foreign firms have expanded their production facilities *within* the United States; investments by Japanese auto firms are an especially important case. This greater foreign direct investment in the United States is, in fact, a significant component of the rising U.S. obligation to foreign interests.

The process I described earlier (Chapter 2) whereby U.S. firms have been losing their preeminence in several sectors has been given a new boost by the financial situation of the 1980s. Of particular importance, the great U.S. debt and trade deficit had its counterpart in the huge Japanese trade surplus and the corresponding expansion of the international role of the Japanese banks. For 1987, *Business Week* (27 June 1988) reported that among the world's largest banks (ranked by assets), the 5 largest, 7 of the top 10, and

21 of the top 50 were Japanese. Citibank ranked number 7, Chase Manhattan 32, and only 2 other U.S. banks made the top 50. The rising role of Japanese banks not only means more profits for them and less for their U.S. rivals. It also gives the Japanese a greater role in affecting the structure of international financial arrangements. For example, during early 1989, when the Bush administration began to offer new proposals—or at least a new rhetoric—for dealing with third world debt, Japanese banks and the Japanese government were playing a larger role than in earlier years. In these and other matters, the U.S. government and U.S. banks still play the most important role, but the rise of Japanese banks is placing new constraints on them.*

Finally, the huge U.S. foreign debt, like the debt of third world countries, creates problems because it must be paid back. Foreign investors, whether they have purchased government securities or private bonds, land in California or office buildings in New York, expect to reap a return. Their investments are a claim on future income in the United States. In one way or another, in the coming years the U.S. economy, like the Latin American economies, must adjust so that resources can be sent out of the country to provide the returns on these investments. But to say that the economy must "adjust" is to say that people must bear a burden. In some combination, U.S. workers will receive lower wages and U.S. corporations will earn lower profits; the U.S. government will make more interest payments and collect more taxes (from whom?) or provide less services (to whom?). The nature of this combination—which groups will bear the bur-

---

*When the U.S. government brokered the new accord between the banks and the Mexican government in July 1989, the banks agreed to a limited reduction in Mexico's debt because "a system of guarantees would assure that the remaining payments on the loan would be made" (*New York Times*, 25 July 1989). It was the Japanese who joined the IMF and the World Bank as the outside guarantors.

den of adjustment—will be a source of major struggle for many years.*

In fact, the struggle has already begun, and its watchword is "austerity." As in Latin America, we in the United States are being told that we must bear the burden for the profligacy of the 1980s. Of course, little attention is given to the question of who made the decisions about, and benefited from, this profligacy. A period of crisis, after all, does not bring an era of logic; it brings an era of political conflict. As with economic problems in general, the U.S. international debt is a political problem and it will be resolved, for better or worse, through a political struggle.†

---

*The situation would be different if the foreign debt were being used—as it generally was in the nineteenth century—to expand the productive capacity of the U.S. economy. Foreign debt does not create a burden if it is used to create a future flow of goods and services that can be used to pay back the principle and interest. But in the U.S., as in Latin America, foreign debt in the late twentieth century does not appear to have been the foundation for rapid growth. Instead, some of it is contributing to the general speculative binge in the United States, the leveraged buyouts that have become the peculiarity of the era. Some simply replaces domestic funds, as is indicated by the extremely low domestic savings rate during the 1980s.

†While the parallels to the third world debt are real, there is a major difference between the U.S. debt and the third world debt. Third world countries owe their debt in foreign currencies, but the United States owes its debt in its own currency. This means that the United States always has the technical option of inflating its debt away, paying off foreign investors with cheap dollars. Such an option certainly has its difficulties: surges of inflation can be very problematic in themselves. Yet it is a factor that distinguishes the U.S. debt, and it is a political option that can always become relevant.

5

Is There an Alternative to Austerity in Latin America?

In Latin America, the debt crisis has created an era of austerity. Governments, in their effort to pay the debt, have cut social programs and restrained economic growth. The result has been not only extreme hardship for the masses of the people, but also a general economic decline and instability that threaten those in power.

Between 1980 and 1987, per capita consumption in the Latin American and Caribbean region fell by 5 percent. In countries where poverty and suffering were already severe, this dry statistic translates into daily misery for millions of people. The future holds little promise of improvement, for, as resources have been transferred abroad to pay the debt, investment in the region has fallen by 27 percent in the 1980 to 1987 period. Without investment—without new factories, schools, roads, farm equipment, health facilities—there is no reason to expect a resurgence of economic growth. [1]

Bad times for the people of Latin America have not meant good times for business. During the 1980s, the major debtor countries of the region have been turning over some 5 percent of national income to foreign creditors. The cost of such a huge transfer cannot be confined to the bottom segments of society. Without economic growth in Latin America, it is hard to conceive where profit can come from.

So why do the governments of debtor nations generally

continue to meet their repayment schedules with the banks? And why do the people of the debtor nations generally accept the austerity programs imposed upon them so that the debt can be paid?

So far governments of capitalist countries in Latin America have failed to offer any alternative to austerity and have attempted to solve their economic problems by relatively orthodox means. They have in general attempted to shape programs that would allow them to pay the debt. All profess a desire for economic growth and an improvement of living standards, but judged by their actions it would seem that all accept that domestic concerns must be subordinated to the continued payment of the debt. Despite a great deal of rhetoric, there has only been limited action to challenge the absolute necessity of paying the debt—Bolivia suspended debt payments in 1985 and has been in a state of de facto if not de jure default since; Peru has severely limited its payments, and even some of the large debtors have fallen behind on their obligations. These actions, however, have been presented as only temporary and limited responses to emergency conditions.*

Heterodox Austerity[2]

Many would challenge the generalization that the Latin American governments have used orthodox means to deal

---

*In early 1989 it might have seemed that the situation was changing—or that the emergency was worsening. According to the *Wall Street Journal* (24 April 1989), "Some heavily indebted countries are increasingly in arrears on their loans, particularly because new conventional bank lending seems more difficult—or even impossible—to obtain." The article mentions Venezuela, Argentina, Ecuador, Peru, Costa Rica, and "other Central American countries" as being in arrears. Being in arrears, however, is not the same as being in default.

with their problems. In several countries during the 1980s economic reform programs were presented as "new alternatives" and were referred to by economists as "heterodox programs." The economic reforms introduced in Argentina during 1985 and in Brazil during 1986 provide the best examples. In each case, programs introduced by post-military elected governments departed from the sort of orthodoxy usually imposed by the International Monetary Fund.

The differences between IMF orthodoxy and this new "heterodoxy" were important ones. Nonetheless, both approaches shared a fundamental commitment to paying the debt. Both were orthodox in that they defined the problem as one of finding a way to pay the debt and to solve domestic economic problems simultaneously. Paying the debt meant continuing to transfer a large amount of resources out of Latin America into the hands of bankers in the United States, Europe, and Japan. To one degree or another, this meant austerity.

These "heterodox" programs were dominated by a concern with inflation. In Argentina, prices had risen by 164 percent, 344 percent, and 627 percent during the three years preceding the program's implementation, and were rising at an annual rate of close to 700 percent when the reform was enacted in late 1985. In Brazil, the three years before the program's introduction had seen price increases of 142 percent, 197 percent, and 227 percent. Inflation was viewed as both a principal symptom and a cause of economic instability. The basic idea behind the new policies was that if inflation could be controlled, the economies would begin to expand.

The most striking common feature of the programs was monetary reform, involving the substitution of a new currency for the old money—the *austral* for the *peso* in Argentina and the *cruzado* for the *cruseiro* in Brazil. The monetary reforms were designed as dramatic moves that would put the governments in a position to greatly reduce the rate of growth of their countries' money supplies. Both programs also included moves to reduce government spending so as to reduce the government deficit.

Where these programs departed from IMF orthodoxy was in the imposition of wage and price controls. These controls involved direct government intervention in the economy and thus a rejection of reliance on unfettered markets. Moreover, their introduction was accompanied by a commitment, at least in rhetoric, to limiting the impact of the austerity measures upon the poor. In Brazil, for example, the new program promised that the government would guarantee the supply of basic food staples.

The Argentinean and Brazilian programs represented a change in Latin America. Reliance on the free market and the ideology of monetarism had been on the rise in the region, but adoption of the new programs represented an upsurge of developmentalist ideology. Developmentalism rejects the "devil take the hindmost" approach of monetarism and the IMF because it is so destructive. The devastation wrought by monetarist policies—for example, in Chile and Argentina during the 1970s—meant extensive bankruptcies and the threat of serious social turmoil. Never accepted in Brazil, even by the military governments, monetarism now seems to be on the defensive in much of Latin America.

The conflict betwen monetarism and developmentalism in Latin America parallels the conflict between monetarism and Keynesianism in the United States. Each represents a significantly different approach, both on the practical and the ideological levels, to how capitalist economies should be run. Neither, however, calls into question the basic principles of capitalism, and in Latin America this means that neither calls into question the basic commitment to pay the debt.

Despite high hopes, the heterodox programs in Argentina and Brazil had little success, bringing about only a very brief and limited reduction in the rate of inflation. In Argentina, inflation rates were somewhat subdued in 1986 and 1987, running at about 100 percent in each of these years. In 1988, however, prices rose by close to 500 percent, and in early 1989 rates of 30 percent to 40 percent per month were reported. (A rate of 40 percent per month amounts to over 5,000 percent per year!) In Brazil, the situation was not substantially different, and by 1988 inflation appears to have been running at around 1,000 percent per year. Likewise, the heterodox programs attained some short-run success with regard to economic growth, but as early as 1987 national output in both countries was rising only at about the rate of population growth.[3]

As far as wages were concerned, the "heterodoxy" of the Argentinean and Brazilian programs did not prove to be an alternative to traditional orthodoxy. In Argentina, real wages fell by between 5 and 10 percent in each year from 1985 through 1987. In Brazil, wages stabilized in the year in which the new program was introduced, but in 1987 they fell by some 25 percent. Although more recent data are not available, there is little doubt but that as inflation has accelerated, real wages have suffered.

Thus with the old orthodoxy and the new heterodoxy, the fundamental problem is the same. When 5 to 10 percent of national income is transferred out of the country to meet debt obligations, as is the case in much of Latin America, resources are simply not available for domestic needs. Economic growth cannot be maintained; nor can the competing demands of different social classes be met. In such circumstances, governments tend to respond with fiscal stimulation and subsidies to various programs, thus attaining some spurts of growth and the short-run satisfaction of demand. But when huge amounts of resources are being transferred abroad, the only way to finance these government outlays is through expansion of the money supply—in effect, by running the printing presses. The result is all but inevitable: acceleration of inflation, instability, and another round of recession.

The Default Option

Yet, even within the social and political framework that prevails in most of Latin America, one can certainly conceive of real alternatives. The option of defaulting appears, at least on the surface, particularly attractive. Brazil and Mexico each make annual debt-service payments of about $12 billion, and Argentina's $7 billion per year is even larger in relation to the size of its economy. Table 5 shows the total debt-service payments of these three countries during the mid-1980s, along with the volume of their imports. It is clear that defaulting would release huge quantities of funds that could be used to expand much needed imports and provide a basis for growth.

Debtor nations have defaulted before. The crisis of the 1930s led to defaults by virtually every country in Latin America.[4] In the current crisis, the Cuban government as well as many nationalists—both those of the left and others—have advocated a cessation of debt payments. Why do the governments of Latin America abjure such action?

Default is sometimes viewed as an unreasonable alternative because creditors could supposedly impose extremely costly sanctions on a defaulter. However, Anatole Kaletsky, a correspondent for London's *Financial Times,* has argued convincingly that in fact sanctions do not constitute a deterrent to default. Kaletsky's position, set out in an important book entitled *The Costs of Defaults,* merits considerable attention, both for the strengths and limits of his analysis.[5]

Table 5
Argentina, Brazil, and Mexico:
Debt Service and Imports, Mid-1980s
(billions of dollars).

	(1) Debt-service actually paid	(2) Imports	(3) Ratio of (1) to (2)
Argentina (1983–86)	29.3	16.1	1.82
Brazil (1983–87)	62.0	71.5	0.87
Mexico (1983–87)	62.6	56.8	1.10

Source: Inter-American Development Bank, *Economic and Social Progress in Latin America: 1988 Report* (Washington, D.C., 1988), pp. 328, 360, 456.

To begin with, Kaletsky points out that, were default to take place, the banks could achieve little if anything through the judicial process. Chase Manhattan cannot foreclose on Brazil in the same way that a local bank can seize the car of a delinquent debtor. Even though most international loans are signed subject to the laws of either the United States or Britain, the courts provide very limited recourse for a bank in its actions against a sovereign defaulter. The doctrine of "sovereign immunity," by which governments could not be sued even for their commercial activities, has been modified in recent decades, but only to a limited extent. In important cases, courts have ruled that to pass judgment on acts of a foreign state would encroach on the making of foreign policy, a function outside the role of the judiciary. And in at least one case, where the foreign debtor was a private concern, the court ruled that default resulted from the acts of a foreign sovereign and refused to make a judgment in favor of the creditors.

Moreover, the "veil of incorporation" protects the assets of state-controlled enterprises with their own legal—i.e., corporate—identities from being held responsible for the debts of their governments. For example, a shipping company that is wholly subject to the control of a debtor government could not, if it were a legal entity in its own right, have its ships confiscated in order to fulfill the obligations of its government to foreign banks. Also, a defaulting country could arrange for its exports to become the property of the buyer before they crossed its own border. Kaletsky provides the example of Mexican oil exports which become the legal property of a foreign purchaser the moment they pass into the customer's tanker.

Legal doctrine in this area remains in flux, and some of the legal decisions noted above are being contested. There is, however, no reason to believe that the potential of legal action by creditors is sufficient to dissuade governments from defaulting.

Kaletsky also dismisses the idea that commercial sanctions imposed by private interests—the banks in alliance with other corporations—would be an effective deterrent to default. Default would not mean the abrogation of all financial and commercial relations, and there is little likelihood that foreign enterprises that are not directly harmed by a default will join in an action against a government that defaults on its debts to the banks. Past cases of default and even nationalization have not brought any effective imposition of private commercial sanctions. As Kaletsky notes, "Managers of multinational companies point out that bankers have rarely refused to do business with countries which had expropriated industrial, oil or mining companies—for example, in Libya, the Middle East, Peru and even Cuba" (p. 33).

Indeed, were default to recreate a basis for economic expansion in Latin America, many multinational firms would probably welcome it, in spite of public protestations to the contrary. Growth would mean market expansion which, after all, has been the primary attraction for multinationals operating in Latin America. Even the banks would not want to give up their lucrative local operations in Brazil just because the Brazilian government defaulted on its international loans. During the early 1980s, Citicorp, the example cited by Kaletsky, was earning over 20 percent of its worldwide profits in Brazil, with a net return on assets five times the U.S. level.

There is of course the danger that default would make it impossible for a country to obtain new loans, not because of organized sanctions but simply because it would be viewed as a bad risk in international capital markets. While the specter of being cut off from international capital markets may have inhibited defaulters prior to 1982, it is hardly a credible threat today. To a very large degree the debtor nations of Latin America have *already* been cut off from capital markets. New loans have been forthcoming in recent years to finance payments on old loans, but there has been virtually no net increase in total funds provided.

The most serious potential problem for defaulting nations would therefore not lie in the realm of private action, whether judicial or nonjudicial, actively planned or simply through the willy-nilly operation of the market. The real question, as Kaletsky emphasizes, is what the reaction of the creditor governments—particularly the U.S. government—would be. There are of course many things that the U.S. and other governments could do, ranging from curtailing trade with the defaulting nation to military intervention. Yet there is little reason to believe that any such action would be taken.

Writing in the age of Reagan, Kaletsky may have been overly sanguine in his assertion that "the use of armed might against a defaulter is unthinkable today" (p. 39). Nonetheless, it is hard to imagine that even the hawks who currently control policy in Washington would attempt an invasion of Argentina, Brazil, or Mexico in response to a default. It is likely, however, that there would be a small chorus raised in Congress for some sort of action—trade restrictions or aid cut-offs, for example. Yet those who carry out foreign policy would be unlikely to view the U.S. "national interest" as well served by the implementation of sanctions. The government would probably view its primary task as one of containing the default, of preventing it from disrupting the international financial system and from threatening other economic interests, such as those of the industrially based multinationals operating in the defaulting nation. Escalating political conflict through sanctions would be unlikely to serve the end of containment. Modern history certainly supports this view. During the last sixty years, since the end of the era of "dollar diplomacy," governments of the advanced capitalist countries have generally taken no action in response to defaults by debtor nations.

Moreover, a defaulting government could act in a way that would minimize the likelihood of retaliation. Kaletsky argues that the government of a debtor nation could undertake a "conciliatory default." The defaulter could act in the least confrontational manner, declaring that its actions were forced on it by circumstances and did not represent any rejection in principle of its economic responsibilities. Also, the default need not include all categories of loans. Debts owed directly to other governments and short-term trade-financing debts could be honored, while long-term private loans would go into default. If this were the case, the likelihood of sanctions, already extremely low in Kaletsky's view, would be reduced even further.

Kaletsky's analysis leads to the conclusion that it is in the interest of governments in debtor nations to default. What's more, Kaletsky argues that those who make policy in the debtor nations will probably reach the same conclusion, and thus "a default . . . appears quite likely in the foreseeable future" (p. 64).

Why Not Default?

Kaletsky's book was published in 1985, and there has as yet been no effective refutation of his arguments. Although we might extend "the foreseeable future" a good deal further, there have so far—with the possible exception of Bolivia—been no true defaults.* Although a new Argentinean president came to power in the summer of 1989 on the basis of radical rhetoric, his government's first action was to impose an austerity program that was hailed by IMF officials. And while the Mexican government used rhetoric that implied a willingness to default if it did not receive substantial concessions from the banks, it accepted a new accord in July 1989 which offered only a limited reduction in its obligations. Likewise, government officials in Brazil, Venezuela, and elsewhere in the region rail against their creditors, but none takes action; none moves to default. Why not?

Even if a default were to occur at this point—and of course one could occur at any point—it would still be necessary to explain why the governments of debtor countries have so far been reluctant to default. Kaletsky's argument and the history the 1930s and earlier eras would lead us to believe that

---

*Bolivia, the poorest nation in Spanish America at the beginning of the 1980s, stopped paying its debts in 1985 after its national income fell 27 percent in four years. (Note, however, that the data do not reflect the income from the cocaine industry.) This extreme disruption made payment of the debt virtually impossible, and in this sense the cessation of payments was hardly a choice. It is significant, however, that Bolivia did not begin payments again even when its economy was somewhat stabilized in the late 1980s. Other countries, as I have noted, have quietly fallen behind in the payment of their debts, and some have announced suspension of payments. So far, however, these steps have been temporary, and governments have picked up on their payments within a short period—often after the delay or suspension resulted in new loans from the IMF, the banks, or the U.S. government.

there should have been at least some defaults by this point in the debt crisis.

I think there are three mutually supporting explanations for why Latin American governments have been reluctant to default, and for why they have attempted to deal with the debt crisis through relatively orthodox means.

The first of these explanations concerns the particular nature of today's debt as compared to the debt of the 1930s. In the 1930s, when much of the third world debt was in the form of bonds that were widely dispersed among private individuals in the advanced countries, there was no real option but to default when a government could not meet its payments. There was no mechanism by which the many bondholders could be organized to negotiate a rescheduling. Today, with the debt highly concentrated in the hands of large multinational banks, negotiated reschedulings are much more readily organized. Thus there are alternatives to outright default that did not exist in the 1930s. Also, the concentration of the debt today means that the potential consequences of default for the international financial system could be much more severe. I will return to this point shortly.*

A second explanation for the reluctance to default emerges from a closer look at Kaletsky's argument. Kaletsky accepts the concept of "national interest," and argues that it is in the national interest of the debtor country to default. The problem is that in class societies there is no such thing as *the* national interest. What is important in explaining the actions of a government on any particular issue is the interests of the dominant class or classes. On the matter of alternative

---

*As a secondary loan market has developed and banks have sold some of their third world debt at discounted rates, the situation has become more like that of the 1930s. Nonetheless, the large banks still hold a large share of the debt.

ways to deal with the debt crisis, it would appear that the orthodox programs being followed in Latin America serve one set of interests, those of the ruling groups.

Even though businesses in Latin America are experiencing hardship, the private wealth and the incomes of rich individuals have not suffered greatly. In his last speech before leaving office at the end of 1982, Mexican President José López Portillo made this point when he referred to poor enterprises with rich entrepreneurs. From Mexico particularly, but also from other large debtor countries in Latin America, there has been a huge flight of capital to safe havens in the advanced countries, particularly in the United States. Thus wealthy Latin Americans have protected themselves against the crisis by holding foreign assets. Also, as adjustment programs have devalued Latin American currencies, the value of these foreign assets measured in terms of home currencies has risen sharply. Rich Latin Americans have not totally disconnected themselves from the fortunes of their enterprises, but they have succeeded in insulating themselves—and have perhaps even gained—from the adjustment process.

In addition, the adjustment process in Latin America may serve a positive long-run function from the point of view of capital. Governments throughout the region are rolling back costly social programs and pushing wage rates through the floor. Organized labor appears ineffective in the face of this onslaught and is likely to suffer a long-run loss of political strength. Thus the debt crisis is providing a convenient rationale for an offensive by capital. The approach is by no means an automatic winner: attempting to create a basis for expansion in this way runs the risk of precipitating a worse crisis. Yet it is an approach that has obvious attractions for capital. (We should note the similarity to the approach taken by U.S. capital during the 1980s.)

A third explanation for the reluctance to default lies in the larger implications of such actions. A default would threaten a possible international financial collapse, which would do drastic harm to the system generally and to the defaulting nation as well. Of course a default, even by a Mexico or Brazil, would not necessarily precipitate a financial collapse. The U.S. government and the governments of the other creditor nations have the means to provide the banks with the funds necessary to prevent collapse. Yet the injection of such funds would itself be disruptive to international finance, and there is always the possibility that the central powers would not act sufficiently rapidly and appropriately. So the first line of defense against international financial turmoil is the prevention of default.

Kaletsky's analysis does not ignore the possibility of international financial turmoil. Yet he apparently believes that such larger concerns are beyond the scope of third world rulers. He approaches their actions with an economism that focuses on direct and tangible costs and benefits while ignoring larger interests.

We can, I think, better understand the actions of Latin American ruling groups if we view them as junior partners in the operation of international capitalism. They do not have the same global responsibilities as their counterparts in the imperial centers, but they do share in the burdens, and benefits, of power. The well-developed complex of ties to international business, of rewards through military and development aid, and of direct political pressure has integrated them into an imperial system and taught them that it serves their own larger interests to avoid disruptive action.

The situation with regard to maintaining the system is substantially different from what it was in the 1930s. The different nature of the debt, as noted above, means that default today would be more likely to be disruptive. While default in the 1930s was costly for those who held the bonds, today default would directly threaten the viability of the major banks. Through the banks the impact of default could spread, and have rapid and deleterious effects on the general availability of credit.

Also, the ruling groups in Latin America today have a different relation to international capitalism than they did in the 1930s. In that earlier period, the Latin American state was not a modern capitalist state but represented an alliance of traditional landed groups, the commercial elite, the semi-autonomous military, and the distinctly junior and emerging industrial capitalist class. The Latin American state was a subordinate state within the international system and operated in alliance with foreign capital, but it was also separate from that system, representing the dominant interests in a society that was still being integrated into the world capitalist order.

The half century since that earlier round of defaults has seen dramatic changes in the sociopolitical structure of Latin American states and in the relation of these states to international capitalism. Especially in the large nations of the region—most obviously Brazil, Mexico, Argentina, and Venezuela—the state has become much more capitalist. Accordingly, the relation with international capital has been more firmly and completely entrenched.*

Capitalism or Barbarism or . . .?

The reluctance of Latin American governments to default is, then, not so unreasonable. There may still be defaults; the

---

*I might add that the officials of these Latin American governments play their roles all the more effectively because so many of them have been trained in U.S. universities. Latin American economists want to maintain their relations with their former professors and other U.S. colleagues, and, with few exceptions, the U.S. economics profession embraces "responsibility" in international financial affairs.

debt crisis is far from over. Yet we should expect that the dominant groups in Latin America will continue to pursue "alternatives" that remain within the confines of accepting both the debt and the austerity that goes with it. What remains to be explained is why the peoples of Latin America continue to tolerate the austerity.

Of course, to some extent the peoples of Latin America do *not* continue to tolerate the austerity. Especially in Brazil and Mexico, the powerful electoral opposition movements that appeared in the late 1980s have their roots in the economic turmoil of the debt crisis, and high on their list of demands is repudiation of the debt. Likewise, in Argentina and elsewhere, the opposition has grown on the basis of a rhetoric of debt renunciation. The increasing strength of these movements has altered debt politics in Latin America. Existing governments and, as I noted in Chapter 1, their patrons in Washington, have begun to search for new ways to handle the debt crisis. Insofar as there is to be any change that will ease the burden on the peoples of Latin America, it will be a result of this new oppositional power rather than of some newfound magnanimity by bank executives or government officials.

Still, despite the magnitude of the economic crisis and despite their growing strength, none of the opposition movements has brought substantial change in their country's debt relations. In several countries of the region, the military has relinquished power to civilian governments and formal democracy has been established, but there has been no further movement toward greater social and economic equality or toward new relations of social and economic power. In general, the masses still bear the burden of austerity.

Economic downturns do not lead to a progressive opposition in the way that turning the tap starts the flow of water. In fact, under some circumstances, as things get worse working people may become less ready to protest. In early 1986, for example, the Argentinean unions organized in the

Confederación General de Trabajo (CGT) called a general strike in Buenos Aires to protest the austerity imposed by the government's "heterodox" program. When the strike failed, *Latin American Weekly Report* (11 April 1986) offered this explanation from a private-sector manager: "It has been a hard time for workers; since the Austral was introduced they have seen their wages reduced by 20 percent, and they do not want to lose their attendance bonus now."

For a popular opposition to develop, people need to believe that a viable alternative exists, not simply in the sense of an alternative economic program but in the sense of an alternative political force. Where civilian regimes have held sway—particularly in Mexico—the ruling groups have successfully used bureaucratic control combined with selective repression to proscribe the emergence of any popular alternative. In those countries where military regimes have held power for extended periods, particularly in Argentina and Brazil, the experience has been especially effective in limiting popular conception of an alternative. Instead of viewing protest as the route to a progressive economic program, many are undoubtedly afraid of a return to military rule. Governments are not unaware of this fear. When Argentina's CGT attempted its action against the government in 1986, the interior minister "reminded the public that confrontations of the sort pursued by the CGT had led to the ouster [by the military], in 1966, of President Arturo Illia."[6]

The history of military rule not only provides current governments with an effective lever for persuading people that their austerity programs are the best that can be hoped for. In addition, military regimes destroyed or greatly weakened the progressive opposition. Whether this took the form of murder and disappearances or simply harassment and severe restrictions of left political activity, the military successfully limited the extent to which the left is a viable alternative political force today.

Thus on the one hand people see elected regimes with their austerity programs. On the other hand, they have lived through the brutality and economic hardship of military rule. The choice then appears as one between the current austerity or a return to military rule: capitalism or barbarism.

This is not a counsel of despair. It is a recognition of the objective limits that face the opposition forces that began to emerge in the late 1980s. Change often comes much faster than we would anticipate in an era of economic crisis, but it is seldom effective when it is simply a spontaneous response to the economic hardship caused by the crisis. In Mexico and Brazil, powerful, progressive opposition movements provide a new basis to hope for substantial political struggle and change. In both these countries, as elsewhere in the region, it is helpful to recognize that economic circumstances per se do not generate a progressive response. As many opposition activists in Latin America are well aware, success will depend on a long period of organizing and building a movement. There is an alternative to austerity only if it is politically created.

6

International Debt and Progressive Politics

In the United States, as in Latin America, the economic turmoil associated directly and indirectly with the international debt has altered the terrain of politics. While the international debt itself does not play the dominant political role here that it does in the third world, it nonetheless hangs like a dark cloud over discussions of foreign and economic policy. The Latin American debt, for example, affects U.S. trade policy, and it is, as I shall point out shortly, tied to U.S. policies of political-military intervention. Moreover, third world debt and the U.S. international debt figure prominently in the determination of macroeconomic policy, affecting actions on interest rates and federal spending. These actions ultimately have their impact on jobs, housing, health, schools, and, indeed, on every aspect of our economic lives. International debt issues do not stand alone in shaping the economic and therefore the political environment, but they are certainly of great importance.

However, it is unlikely that the people who run the U.S. government will find a solution to the debt problem. Indeed, as I have argued in the preceding chapters, both the third world debt crisis and the crisis of U.S. international debt have been in large part the products of U.S. government policies, of steps taken in response to the instability and relative stagnation that have been the plague of the international economy for the last two decades. While it is possible that new policies could alter the manifestations of this "plague," a "cure" seems beyond the scope of government action. Furthermore, insofar as U.S. policymakers can find ways to ameliorate international debt problems, their actions will focus on stability, on restoring "order" to the economies of the third world, to international financial markets, and to the foreign debt and trade relationships of the United States. They will not implement programs that will begin to alter the poverty and degradation that is the lot of hundreds of millions in the third world or that will stop the trend toward inequality and insecurity in the United States. "Austerity" is the watchword of policymakers in the United States and in Latin America, and austerity cannot be the foundation for any lasting or desirable solution.

There is, then, a need for opposition political action. Progressive political forces in the United States have been concerned with the third world debt crisis since it first appeared as an issue in the early 1980s, recognizing its connection to conflict between the advanced capitalist countries and the peoples in the system's periphery. Also, although the U.S. debt has not been a focus for political struggle, progressive groups have attempted to formulate ways to oppose the official imposition of austerity and to confront the dislocation and loss of power that workers have experienced as a consequence of changing trade patterns. On trade-related problems, organized labor has been at the center of controversy, both at the local level and on questions of national policy. Accordingly, there have been progressive initiatives to develop policies by which labor can respond to the continuing disruption of international economic relations.

Some Lessons from Experience

But the progressive movement in the United States has not made any great strides in its work on international debt issues. Part of the problem is surely the general weakness of progressive forces in this country, but I think our weakness on international debt issues and, more generally, on international economic issues goes beyond our general weakness.

On the one hand, in presenting international debt as an issue in and of itself, we have been asking people to take up a problem that is distant from their lives and difficult to understand. We have not done enough to connect international debt problems to other political struggles. Consequently, we have foregone the possibility of broadening and strengthening those other struggles and missed the opportunity to focus political action on the international debt.

On the other hand, when we have tied debt and other international issues into a broader progressive agenda, we have often done so by laying out general "programs" that offer progressive alternatives to current government policy. When presenting alternative programs, we can get trapped by the need to provide proposals that appear reasonable within the existing order. Yet in an effort to be "reasonable" we may undermine the foundations of an opposition movement. Also, general programs are limited as practical tools because they do not provide people with solid connections that are relevant in political work.

Examples of some of these problems are provided by the response in the early 1980s of progressive groups to the third world debt crisis. Several people working on international issues formed the Debt Crisis Network and published their analysis and program in a useful book entitled *From Debt to Development: Alternatives to the International Debt Crisis.*[1] The Network's analysis was in many ways similar to that which I have presented in the early chapters of this book; it was highly critical of the practices of the U.S. government and international lending agencies, of the banks, and of the elites who control the governments of third world countries. The group's program was designed to shift the burden of the debt crisis off the backs of the poor and to promote egalitarian economic development.

The Debt Crisis Network has had success as an educational effort, providing many people with a better understanding of the debt crisis and of relations between the United States and the third world. Yet it has not accomplished a great deal in terms of mobilizing popular support for its program or for other political action on the debt.* In part its work has been hampered by the problem that hampers all progressive political action that is defined in terms of a single issue. But international debt is an especially poor single-issue focus for political work. Within the United States, the third world debt issue has no popular constituency. Also, while Latin Americans may view the debt crisis as a "war," it does not strike people in the United States with the same force as do the shooting wars sponsored or engaged in by the U.S. government. Events in Nicaragua and El Salvador in particular have captured the attention of U.S. progressive activists much more readily than has the debt crisis.

The Debt Crisis Network was also caught in the trap that snares many people who attempt to provide programs for dealing with the turmoil created by capitalism. The essence of the Network's original program can be summarized in three points: (1) The IMF should replace its austerity programs with development programs that create jobs, advance basic human needs, create equality, and preserve natural

---

*In discussing the Debt Crisis Network, I do not want to denigrate the group's work. It has played a positive role. Precisely because it has done good work, it provides us with a point of reference. My hope is that through the sort of arguments I raise here it will be possible to build on work like that of the Debt Crisis Network and make it even more effective.

resources for sustainable development. U.S. aid programs should be redirected in a similar manner, and military aid should be cut and replaced with development assistance. (2) Debt-relief programs should be undertaken that would forgive some debt, extend payment periods, and set a ceiling on debt service as a share of a country's export earnings at 20 percent. (3) Government regulation of banks should prevent future massive, unchecked overseas lending, and there should be more meaningful public regulation of banks bailed out by the U.S. government.

While these points certainly appear desirable in themselves, they embody difficulties that are endemic to alternative programs. To begin with, the proposals accept the principle of conditionality in the operations of the IMF. To be sure, they put conditionality not in terms of traditional IMF austerity programs, but in terms of "good" goals that progressives can generally support—more jobs and provision of basic needs. Yet the principle of conditionality, the principle whereby those institutions in the world that control the money impose policies on the poor nations, is not challenged.

In an effort to offer a program that is workable within the existing order of things, the Debt Crisis Network people are constrained to implicitly accept certain rules of the game. They have little choice but to accept the "rule" that the rich nations, the United States in particular, are going to use the wealth and power they have to direct events throughout the world. The global inequality of wealth and power is one of the defining features of our system, and therefore cannot be directly challenged by a "reasonable" program. Yet as I argued earlier, it is this system of wealth and power, the operation of these rules of the game, that lies at the root of the debt crisis.

It is possible to win some victories by advocating programs like those proposed by the Debt Crisis Network. Some funds could be diverted toward more desirable ends. Yet ultimately the approach undermines itself. It does not sufficiently challenge the unequal distribution of wealth and power or the interventionism generated by international inequality. Also, it does not sufficiently alter the terms of the discussion. Despite their belief to the contrary, people who follow this "programs approach" are led away from examining how the system really works.

Advocates of a "programs approach" will sometimes argue that their strategy does educate people about the way the system works. When people in power reject proposals that are socially desirable and reasonable, they demonstrate the limits of the system and its inability to serve human needs. Certainly it is desirable to continually push the system, to make demands on those in power, and to use defeats as well as victories for education. I think we do better, however, not to limit ourselves to demands that are "reasonable" in the sense of accepting the rules of the game. We do better to demand what is desirable in terms of human needs.

The same theme of implicitly accepting the rules of the game appears in other aspects of the Debt Crisis Network program. It proposes that countries limit their debt payments to 20 percent of export earnings. But unless we accept the basic legitimacy of the debt relationship—which means accepting the basic legitimacy of international power relationships—why should the countries pay at all? Why not default? Similarly, the Network advocates that the U.S. government impose new regulations when it bails out banks. But why assume that the government will bail out the banks, that we must rely on large private financial institutions to direct our economic lives? Why accept this as one of the givens of the situation? Again, the problem comes from working within the rules of the game.*

---

*In its more recent work, the Debt Crisis Network has moved beyond its original program, apparently recognizing some of the problems I have noted here. In particular, it has moved to a position of advocating debt repudiation by third world countries.

There are, of course, times when it is desirable for the progressive movement to work within the rules of the game, when doing so allows it to win some immediate and tangible goals. A "purism" that rejects all efforts to make gains within the system is hardly relevant to people's real needs. Yet we must be aware of the problems that come with advocating programs that implicitly accept the rules of the game. When we accept the rules, we tend to legitimize them and thus strengthen them.

I have used the Debt Crisis Network's work to suggest some of the limits of our response to international debt problems in part because the Network experience is in many ways typical of a great deal of progressive political activity. In general, progressive forces have not found ways to make international economic problems relevant to a popular constituency. Indeed, to my knowledge, there has been no effort to develop any progressive response to the development of the huge U.S. foreign debt.

When issues are dealt with, they are often dealt with in isolation, as single-issue problems; this has been true of our approach to foreign trade as well as our approach to third world debt. The single-issue approach to trade has a ready constituency among the workers directly threatened by foreign competition. It is, however, particularly problematic because it often leads into a narrow, traditional protectionism that places workers in the directly affected industries at odds with other workers. Furthermore, as my earlier arguments imply, when foreign trade is taken up as an issue unto itself, no effective solutions are available. An effective response to trade problems has to deal with financial issues, macroeconomic policy, and, indeed, the whole structure of international economic relations.

A principal way in which progressives have moved beyond single-issue politics on foreign and other economic issues has been through the formulation of general economic programs. These programs have had some positive impact. In particular, they can be a useful educational tool, demonstrating that there is a progressive alternative to status quo economic policies. Yet, like the Debt Crisis Network's program, general economic programs are often limited by the need to appear "reasonable." Also, as I have suggested, general programs tend to be too general, failing to provide connections between issues that are immediately relevant to practical progressive struggles; something more concrete is needed.[2]

Building a Progressive Response

There are other ways to build a progressive response to international economic issues, and to debt problems in particular. Considerable useful work can be done that neither treats those issues in isolation nor relies on what I have called the "programs approach." Whether we focus on the third world debt crisis or on the problem of the U.S. foreign debt, our political response can begin by recognizing the connection between these issues and the larger crisis of international capitalism. Debt issues are tied to the operation of U.S. power in the world economy, to U.S. government macroeconomic policies designed to deal with stagnation and instability, to trade policies, and to power relations between capital and labor. These are conclusions that emerge from the analysis I have presented in the preceding chapters, and they should provide a basis for political strategy. Also, the analysis brings out the fact that the principal problems of the international economy have their roots in the way the system operates, in the rules of the game. An effective progressive politics may not be able to overcome or alter these rules in the foreseeable future, but neither should we accept, and thereby reinforce, them as a basis for our actions.

Anti-Intervention Work. The first place where we can take up debt issues is in our continuing anti-intervention work. In fact, anti-intervention work is in effect a response to the third world debt crisis. The debt crisis arose out of inequality and dependency, out of the particular social structures that dominate third world countries, and out of their ties to the international economy. U.S. intervention—political and military, direct and indirect—is designed primarily to preserve the status quo in the third world. Any lasting and desirable solution to the debt crisis requires a break with the status quo. Blocking U.S. intervention thus holds out at least the possibility of supporting solutions to the third world debt crisis.

Consider Nicaragua. The Sandinista government has begun to organize egalitarian and participatory programs that challenge the foreign domination of the country's economic life. It has begun to establish an economy along lines that, as the Debt Crisis Network points out, may provide a solution to the debt crisis—but without any "good" conditionality or support from the IMF. The U.S. government has been trying for years to destroy the Sandinista alternative by conducting CIA sabotage, sponsoring military intervention, and preventing Nicaragua from obtaining development assistance from international agencies. If we allow the Nicaraguan effort to be cut down, how can we continue to talk about the desirability of new alternative programs in Latin America?

For the international banks and the IMF to continue with "business as usual," the power of the U.S. government in international affairs—its ability to dominate the governments of the third world—must be maintained. The U.S. government is, ultimately, the enforcer. Without its power, the whole context of debt and domination would be altered. Thus any meaningful effort to overcome the debt crisis in a progressive manner must challenge U.S. imperialism in its totality. Nicaragua has been a focal point of conflict for several years, and other points of struggle will arise—perhaps, as the debt crisis continues to take its toll, even in such large countries as Brazil and Mexico. We should not view these struggles as something separate from the debt crisis, and we should emphasize that in opposing U.S. intervention we are also supporting attempts to solve international debt problems.

Struggles over Budgetary Priorities and Austerity. Similarly, both third world debt and the U.S. foreign debt should be brought into progressive struggles over the government's budgetary priorities and efforts to impose austerity. A debt problem is always a *distributional* problem, a problem of who will pay. The conflict over who will pay the Latin American debt and who will pay the U.S. foreign debt is obscured, however, because the burdens of payment are often hidden and indirect.

In Latin America, the burden of the debt has so far been primarily borne, clearly and directly, by workers and peasants whose standard of living has been sharply curtailed. The burden can be shifted, however, when either economic collapse or the demands of popular movements threaten to cut off the flow of funds from Latin America to the banks. Then the issue becomes one of whether the banks' owners will be forced to bear the losses, or whether the general public in the United States (and in other advanced countries) will bear the burden, either by providing new funds to the debtor countries or by bailing out the banks. When the public pays, it does so in a variety of indirect ways: through higher taxes, higher interest rates, and a reduction in other government programs. These burdens are often difficult to see. For example, the U.S. government has pursued programs that allow the internationally operating banks to spread losses from third world loans over several years, thus lowering their tax burdens. The lower tax burdens for the banks mean higher tax burdens, or less government services, for the rest of us.*

Paying off the U.S. foreign debt is also a question of who will pay, and the process by which the payment is distributed is at least as complex. As I explained earlier, the U.S. debt problem and the U.S. trade problem are really a single issue, and the burden of the debt appears in the burden of jobs lost and wages suppressed in connection with foreign trade. Because of this connection between debt and trade, U.S. workers bore a high cost as the debt, and the trade deficit, rose. And if the import rate continues at its current high level, U.S. workers will continue to feel the pressure of foreign competition. Also, any move toward reducing the trade gap—and the debt—is likely to come at workers' expense because a relative rise in U.S. exports would be possible only if wages were kept from rising. In addition to adjustments in the private sector, the U.S. foreign debt provides a club for conservative forces to continue to beat away at government social programs. To pay off the foreign debt, or simply to stop it from increasing, the government must reduce its own borrowing, which means reducing the federal deficit. Proposals to reduce the federal deficit quickly become proposals to cut social spending and impose austerity.

Progressive forces are continually involved in struggles over budgetary priorities. Both groups focusing on particular issues and broader coalitions have resisted the effort to balance the budget on the backs of the poor. They are often faced, however, with what appears as the overwhelming and

---

*If the flow of funds from Latin America were cut off, and the banks were not bailed out and allowed to fail, they would not be able to pay off their creditors—people who have deposited money in the banks. Most deposits are insured by government agencies, so even if the government did not save the bank owners, it would still have costs to bear. This means that taxpayers and service recipients would bear the costs, and struggles over the budget would intensify.

negative logic of the larger macroeconomic situation, a situation which, partly because of international debt factors, does not seem to allow their demands to be met. This is a false logic in that it rests on the principle that all adjustments must be made without any disruption of the existing structures of U.S. and international capitalism. For example, major banks on the brink of failure must be bailed out while we rely on them to run the world's financial system, and the government's budgetary options are very limited without any controls on the movement of international funds. Yet these are rules of the game that need not be respected.

By bringing debt issues into struggles over the government's budgetary priorities, we can enhance those struggles and confront debt issues more effectively. Drawing this sort of connection helps build a domestic constituency on international issues. At the same time, it spreads an awareness that particular social crises—crises of health, schooling, and housing, for example—are products of the larger operation of the capitalist economy (an issue of education to which I will return shortly).

Conflicts over Trade and Jobs. The general approach of building struggles by connecting their particular focus to the larger operation of the international economy is also applicable in conflicts over trade and jobs. The trade problem, like the debt problem to which it is bound, cannot be separated from the larger framework of the role of U.S. power in the world economy and from the macroeconomic policies of the government that have evolved in that framework. While workers whose jobs and wages are under attack have, reasonably enough, often responded with demands for protection from imports, their struggles could be more effective if they were broadened.*

---

*One of the problems with protectionism is that it tends to place the directly affected workers in conflict with other workers who, as consumers,

It seems particularly desirable to build trade-related job struggles on the basis of a recognition of the way the huge trade deficit of the 1980s arose. The government, as I have shown, made certain macroeconomic policy choices that generated the trade deficit (and the U.S. foreign debt). Those choices were not "mistakes" but were the product of an effort to maintain U.S. power in the world economy and to enhance the position of business and of the wealthy within the U.S. economy. The trade problems of workers are thus the result of macroeconomic policies and of the grander agenda that generated those policies. Particular protectionist demands— if they are implemented at all—will achieve very limited, short-run gains if the principles of government policy remain intact. If the government is allowed to pursue a policy that is designed to enhance the role of U.S. business in an open world economy, and if business is able to move its funds around the world without restrictions, then there is little hope for protecting workers from the impact of trade shifts. Even when this sort of policy maintains the growth of the national economy, trade shifts will continually present workers with the reality or threat of dislocation—loss of one job and movement to another. As a result, their incomes and power will be undermined.

Anti-intervention work provides one useful mechanism for joining the trade-related concerns of U.S workers to the general issue of U.S. power in the world economy. Efforts by the U.S. government to preserve existing economic and social relations in the third world are part of a larger effort to maintain an open international economy, a situation where business is free to move in search of cheaper labor, less

---

are likely to pay higher prices for goods if imports are limited. Thus when the struggle over trade is undertaken as single-issue politics, it can become a distributional struggle among workers. The most effective way to avoid such division and gain some positive, lasting result is to broaden the struggle over trade to a struggle over jobs and security in general.

environmental regulation, or whatever else may increase profits. People struggling for social and economic change in the third world are the direct victims of our government's actions, but U.S. workers are also weakened by them. While the problem appears in terms of cheap imports coming from the Far East or Latin America, the underlying problem is one of power. The power of U.S. workers is undermined as business gains more international options, and from this fact arises the need to combine job struggles and anti-interventionist struggles.[3]

To return again to the third world debt crisis, here too there is a direct need to combine trade and job struggles with the larger question of international economic policy. Latin America has been a large source of demand for U.S. exports, but during the 1980s that demand dropped dramatically as the region's resources were directed away from imports and into paying the debt. When the debt gets paid and the demand for U.S. exports is directly reduced, some of the funds go through the banks to be re-spent on U.S. goods. Yet it seems most likely that the net effect on U.S. jobs is negative, and surely there is considerable dislocation as some industries lose while others gain. Thus working people in the United States are harmed by government policies that continue to deny debt relief and wring every dollar possible out of the debtor countries.

Educational Work and Ideology

Much of what I have been advocating here boils down to the expansion of progressive educational programs. This is as it should be. The work of organizing people into progressive campaigns is always largely an educational task.

People know the problems they face in their everyday lives, but they are denied the information and experience that enables them to see those problems as part of a larger process and as tied to other people's parallel problems. To move people, to organize them, so they see that the solution to their own problems lies in a general change of society involves a massive educational effort.

On international debt issues as such, there are progressive people doing some of this educational work. Our goal should be to expand this activity so that work on the debt is not confined to single-issue campaigns. Single-issue campaigns can be strategically useful for reaching particular constituencies and for initiating action. Yet progressives always need to be concerned with broadening these campaigns, not by subordinating partcular concerns to some grand vision, but by building on that vision by combining and strengthening the particular concerns. On international debt issues, the need to develop connections is especially important because of the lack of a natural constituency.

One part of progressive educational work on the international debt should be seen as explicitly ideological. Underlying political disputes on economic problems is a fundamental ideological conflict. On the one hand, there are those who argue that capitalism, whatever its difficulties, is basically a system that works, one that reproduces itself from year to year in a satisfactory manner. The problems that arise are then attributed to policy mistakes, bad luck, or irresponsible business practices, not to the way capitalism works as a system. In this view, the solution to economic problems lies in fixing up the system, in making capitalism work better. On the other hand, there are those of us who see capitalism as fundamentally flawed, as a system that does not work in the dual sense that it continually undermines its own operation (the process of growth generates disruption and decline) and that it denies people their basic needs for decent and secure living standards and for creative work. In our view, the opposition view, the solution to our economic problems lies in changing the system and replacing capitalism with a different way of organizing economic life.

There are many ways to advance the opposition view—the nature of work in capitalist society and the insecurity created by cycles of unemployment and inflation, for example, deserve considerable attention. International debt problems, however, offer a special opportunity. These problems reveal how the capitalist system operates in a thoroughly irrational and pernicious manner. The international debt crisis has led to insecurity and misery on a wide scale, not apart from capitalism but closely connected to its most sophisticated business operations. The homeless in São Paulo and Mexico City, as well as in Washington and Los Angeles, are as much a part of the capitalist system as are middle America's suburbanites.

Furthermore, as I have tried to demonstrate in this book, debt problems did not result from government policy "mistakes," from the "bad luck" of shifting oil prices, or from "irresponsible" banking practices. Instead, the debacle of international debt grew out of the normal, though often contradictory, operation of capitalism. U.S. government policies played a particularly important role, to be sure, but those policies were a rational attempt to preserve the power of U.S. business in an era of instability and relative stagnation. Oil prices also played a role, as did the actions of the banks. But these events were not initial causal factors; they were links in a larger process. This larger process was the interplay of economic and political power, acting through the market and through the state. This larger process was the normal operation of capitalism.

The ideological dispute over the way capitalism works or

does not work is important because it affects the way people approach political struggle. If they see their problems as deeply rooted in the nature of our economic and social system, they are more likely to engage in a struggle to change that system.

Notes

1. *International Debt*

1. Inter-American Development Bank, *Economic and Social Progress in Latin America: 1988 Report* (Washington, D.C., 1988 and previous years).
2. Data are from the *Economic Report of the President, 1988*, p. 374.
3. According to David Felix and Juana Sanchez, "Capital Flight Aspects of the Latin American Debt Crisis," Working Paper #106, Department of Economics, Washington University, St. Louis, 1987, foreign assets held by Mexicans and by Argentineans as of 1985 exceeded those countries' levels of foreign debt. For Brazil, Felix and Sanchez estimate that foreign assets constituted 34 percent of that country's foreign debt, a smaller but still substantial figure.
4. Quoted in *Dollars & Sense*, November 1985.
5. These data are all computed from Inter-American Development Bank, *Economic and Social Progress in Latin America, 1988 Report*.
6. Ibid.
7. *Economic Report of the President, 1988*, p. 367.
8. The figures on third world debt are from World Bank *World Debt Tables, External Debt of Developing Countries*, 1988–89 edition, *Volume I. Analysis and Summary Tables* (Washington D.C., 1988), p. x. The figure for 1989 is a preliminary estimate. For the United States, from 1960 to 1980 the ratio of outstanding debt of nonfinancial borrowers to GNP remained very close to 1.4; it had jumped to 1.8 by 1986; see Benjamin Friedman, "Lessons of Monetary Policy from the 1980s," *Journal of Economic Perspectives* 2, no. 3 (Summer 1988): 63–4. The data on the historical increase of the ratio of new net borrowing to GNP

in the United States are taken from Robert Pollin, "Debt-Dependent Growth and Financial Innovation: Instability in the U.S. and Latin America," in Arthur MacEwan and William K. Tabb, eds., *Instability and Change in the World Economy* (New York: Monthly Review Press, 1989), p. 123.

2. U.S. Imperial Decline

1. The GM data are from J. W. Sundelson, "U.S. Automotive Investment Abroad," in Charles P. Kindleberger, *The International Corporation* (Cambridge, MA.: MIT Press, 1970), p. 256. The data on the concentration of foreign earnings are from Thomas E. Weisskopf, "United States Foreign Investment: An Empirical Survey," in Richard C. Edwards, Michael Reich, and Thomas E. Weisskopf, eds., *The Capitalist System* (Englewood Cliffs, N.J.: Prentice-Hall, 1972), p. 433.

2. U.N. Economic Commission for Latin America, *External Financing in Latin America*, 1965, pp. 16–17 and 147–48.

3. United Nations Commission on Transnational Corporations, *Salient Features and Trends in Foreign Direct Investment*, 1983, Table 2, as cited by Peter Dicken, *Global Shift: Industrial Change in a Turbulent World*, (New York: Harper & Row, 1986), Table 3.4.

4. Lawrence Franko, "Multinationals: The End of U.S. Dominance," *Harvard Business Review* (November–December 1978), pp. 95–96.

5. Harry Magdoff and Paul Sweezy, "The End of U.S. Hegemony," *Monthly Review* (October 1971): 8.

6. Robert Triffin, "The International Role and Fate of the Dollar," *Foreign Affairs* 57, no. 2 (Winter 1978/9), esp. p. 270.

7. See Ronald McKinnon, "Currency Substitution and Instability in the World Dollar Standard," *American Economic Review* 72, no. 3 (1982), esp. pp. 320 and 322; and ibid.

8. See J.-P. Koszul, "American Banks in Europe," in Charles P. Kindleberger, ed., *The International Corporation* (Cambridge, MA: MIT Press, 1970).

9. Andrew F. Brimmer and F. A. Dahl, "Growth of International Banking: Implications for Public Policy," *Journal of Finance* (May 1975): 345, and the *Federal Reserve Bulletin*, August 1981, pp. A17 and A54. For a more extensive discussion of the expansion of international banking,

see R. M. Pecchioli, *The Internationalization of Banking: Policy Issues* (Paris: OECD, 1983).

10. Salomon Brothers, Inc., Bank Securities Department, "U.S. Multinational Banking Semiannual Statistics," 22 December 1983, p. 7.

11. See Arthur MacEwan, "Slackers, Bankers, and Marketers: Multinational Firms and the Pattern of U.S. Direct Foreign Investment," A Working Paper, Department of Economics, University of Massachusetts—Boston, May 1982, p. 16; and *Survey of Current Business*, August 1984.

12. *Harpers*, September 1983.

13. The GNP growth rate data are from the *Economic Report of the President, 1988*, p. 374. The investment data are from Organization for Economic Cooperation and Development (OECD), *Main Economic Indicators, Historical Statistics* (Paris, 1979); OECD, *Main Economic Indicators*, March 1982; and *Economic Report of the President, 1984*.

14. See memorandum prepared by Robert H. Mills, Jr. entitled, "Spreads and Maturities on Eurocurrency Credits—Fourth Quarter 1981 and Two-Year Review," Board of Governors of the Federal Reserve System, 3 March 1982, as cited by William Darity, Jr., "Loan Pushing: Doctrine and Theory," *International Finance Discussion Papers*, Number 247, Board of Governors of the Federal Reserve (Washington, D.C., September 1984), p. 12.

3. Dependence and Inequality

1. Celso Furtado, *Economic Development of Latin America: Historical Background and Contemporary Problems* (New York: Cambridge University Press, 1976), p. 23.

2. Stanley J. Stein and Barbara H. Stein, *The Colonial Heritage of Latin America: Essays on Economic Dependence in Perspective* (New York: Oxford University Press, 1970), p. 134.

3. Harry Magdoff, "International Economic Distress and the Third World," *Monthly Review* (April 1982). Magdoff demonstrates clearly a point to which I shall return shortly: that "oil is not the culprit. It is but another weight added to an overwhelmingly larger and older set of burdens, made much worse by the onset of stagnation in the core countries."

4. Ronald E. Müller, "The Multinational Corporation and the Under-

development of the Third World," in Charles Wilbur, ed., *The Political Economy of Development*, 2nd ed. (New York: Random House, 1979), p. 164.

5. Alain de Janvry, *The Agrarian Question and Reformism in Latin America* (Baltimore and London: Johns Hopkins University Press, 1981), pp. 34–35.

6. For details of these relationships in the Brazilian case, see Peter Evans, *Dependent Development: The Alliance of Multinational, State and Local Capital in Brazil* (Princeton, N.J.: Princeton University Press, 1979).

7. See Magdoff, n. 3 above, on the role of oil in affecting Latin America's international accounts.

8. See Frank Ackerman, "Industry and Imperialism in Brazil," *Review of Radical Political Economics* (Spring 1971): 17.

9. See Cheryl Payer, *The Debt Trap: The IMF and the Third World* (New York: Monthly Review Press, 1974).

10. Considerable details on these steps are provided by Myra Wilkins, *The Maturing of Multinational Enterprises: U.S. Business Abroad from 1914 to 1970* (Cambridge, MA.: Harvard University Press, 1974), pp. 353–65.

11. See J.P. Curhan et al., *Tracing the Multinationals: Sourcebook on U.S.-Based Multinationals* (Cambridge, MA: Ballinger Publishing Co., 1977), p. 24.

12. See *Business Week*, 17 May 1982.

13. See Curhan et al., n. 11 above, pp. 178–82.

14. Things do not always work out as they are supposed to, however, and there are sometimes implicit contradictions in the conditionality agreements. For example, in the name of cutting imports, the Mexican government has placed restrictions on imports of pharmaceutical raw materials, putting multinational firms at a disadvantage compared to Mexican firms. See *Business Week*, 1 October 1984.

4. Financial Shift

1. Data are from *Statistical Abstract of the United States*, various years.

2. On the details of U.S. trade patterns in the 1960s and 1970s, see William H. Branson, "Trends in U.S. International Trade and Invest-

ment Since World War II," in Martin S. Feldstein, ed., *The American Economy in Transition* (Chicago: University of Chicago Press, 1980).

3. Details of the trade balance are computed from data in *Statistical Abstract of the United States*, various years.

4. *Economic Report of the President, 1986*, p. 373; *1988*, p. 371. There is dispute over the statistical procedures used in constructing the overall "trade-weighted" real value of the dollar. The dispute, however, centers on the speed of the decline in the value of the dollar after 1985, and no one seems to deny the general trend up to 1985. Also, the late 1970s did constitute a low point in the value of the dollar over the past twenty years.

5. Is There an Alternative to Austerity?

1. The numbers are from Inter-American Development Bank, *Economic and Social Progress in Latin America: 1988 Report* (Washington D.C., 1988).

2. Data referred to in this section are, unless otherwise indicated, from ibid.

3. The 1988 inflation figures are estimates taken from Eliana A. Cardoso, "Hyperinflation in Latin America," *Challenge* 32, no. 1 (January/February 1989), Table 1.

4. The defaults of the 1930s were nothing new. Clifford Dammers traces defaults on international debt back to the 4th century B.C. and notes: "In 1327 the English King, Edward III, renounced his debts to Italian bankers and the Bardi and Peruzzi banks subsequently failed. From the sixteenth to nineteenth century, France ceased payments on its debts on the average of once every thirty years." (See "A Brief History of Sovereign Defaults and Rescheduling," in David Suratgar, ed., *Default and Rescheduling: Corporate and Sovereign Borrowers* [Washington, D.C.: Euromoney Publications, 1984], p. 77.) It was, however, in the nineteenth century, with the great expansion of world capitalism, that both international lending and then defaults increased substantially. (See Peter H. Lindert and Peter J. Morton, "How Sovereign Debt Has Worked," in Jeffrey D. Sachs, ed., *Developing Country Debt and Economic Performance* [Chicago: University of Chicago Press, 1989].) Lindert and Morton provide a lengthy country-by-country list in a table

entitled "A Summary of Default and Rescheduling on Government Debt to Foreign Countries Since 1820."

5. Anatole Kaletsky, *The Costs of Default* (New York: The Twentieth Century Fund, 1985).
6. *Latin American Weekly Report,* 14 March 1986.

6. International Debt and Progressive Politics

1. Debt Crisis Network, *From Debt to Development: Alternatives to the International Debt Crisis* (Washington, D.C.: Institute for Policy Studies, 1986). The Debt Crisis Network also publishes *U.S. Debt Crisis Network Newsletter,* Suite 520, 1400 I Street NW, Washington, D.C. 20005.
2. In the early 1980s, left economists produced various such programs. Good examples are those in: Samuel Bowles, David M. Gordon, and Thomas E. Weisskopf, *Beyond the Wasteland: A Democratic Alternative to American Decline* (Garden City, N.Y.: Anchor Press/Doubleday, 1983); Gar Alperovitz and Jeff Faux, *Rebuilding America* (New York: Pantheon Books, 1984); and Martin Carnoy, Derek Shearer, and Russell Rumberger, *A New Social Contract: The Economy and Government After Reagan* (New York: Harper & Row, 1983). In more recent years, perhaps because the left has become more used to its distant relationship to power, there have been fewer programmatic proposals.
3. See David Slaney, "Thinking Globally: Labor Rights Legislation and El Salvador," *Dollars & Sense* (May 1989), on the way progressive activists in the U.S. labor movement have used existing international labor rights legislation as a lever in developing opposition to the U.S. government's foreign policy. El Salvador has received particular attention.

Index

143